The Original
LOVERS'
QUESTIONNAIRE
Book

Written and Illustrated
by
Lorilyn Bailey

L♦O♦R♦M♦A♦X
Communications
Raleigh, North Carolina
United States of America

The Original **LOVERS' QUESTIONNAIRE** Book

♥

Copyright ©1995 Lorilyn Bailey

ISBN 0-9641239-9-1

Published in the United States by
LORMAX Communications
PO Box 40304
Raleigh, NC 27629-0304

♥

NOTE: The numbered statements
in this book do not necessarily
reflect the views of the author or publisher.
The statements presented are used as a tool to
identify opinions and stimulate discussion.
Specific information on the topics may be found at your
local library or bookstore.

♥

Cover design and photography by Lorilyn Bailey

♥

Author photo by Glamour Shots

Table of Contents

Dedication

To couples everywhere who believe in true love.

WHY YOU NEED THIS BOOK

If you want to know more about your partner's values, you've taken the right step in selecting this book. But that's not the only benefit you'll gain. You will have an opportunity — perhaps the first one you've ever had — to identify:

- ♥ Your own beliefs on many subjects
- ♥ Your areas of compatibility
- ♥ Your areas of incompatibility.

The *greatest* benefit you'll gain is that you will find it easier to sit down and discuss the many issues that you need to discuss as a couple. Such discussions *may* help your relationship grow into a mutually satisfying and long-lasting union.

Although this book is intended primarily for unmarried couples, married couples may enjoy answering the questions and may discover new information about each other.

You will be presented with more than five hundred statements in twenty-six different topic areas. You will indicate whether you agree or disagree with the statements. By comparing your responses, you will identify those areas in which your beliefs match and where they differ.

If you are honest in answering the questions in this book, you will be able to identify your areas of incompatibility. You can better resolve (or prevent) problems if you have first *identified* them.

Think of those incompatible areas as small bumps in the road of life. By identifying what's ahead, you can discuss your options. You may wish to slow down, take an alternate route, or hit those bumps head on. You may decide to skip the trip. However, you may feel confident that you'll enjoy the challenge of overcoming the obstacles on the road to happiness.

What's In This Book?

This book is divided into three sections:

I.   The Basics: Beliefs, Preferences, Habits, and Health
II.   The Great Debates: Commonly Argued Topics
III.   The Future

Within each of these sections are several topics, and they are listed in the table of contents at the front of the book.

Don't expect to find out *everything* about your partner with this book. This book does not ask details about your partner's former loves — or their *entire* health and financial histories. Everyone is entitled to some privacy, and as your relationship grows, you will discover much about your partner's beliefs and desires. However, this book does bring up the ***important*** issues that may affect **you** and **your relationship**.

This book *does* include questions about a person's mental health history. If you find your potential partner is undergoing therapy and medication for a problem, that should be a *plus*. It means the person has admitted he or she needed some help (as **many** people do) and were intelligent and strong enough to obtain that help.

Keep in Mind

This is not a typical self-analysis book. You will **not** tabulate your scores at the end to determine into which little category you might fit. There are no right or wrong answers. After you and your partner complete the questionnaire, you interpret your own answers. It is up to *you* to determine the type of person with whom you wish to spend your time.

Why I Wrote This Book

The experts tell us that half of all marriages these days end in divorce, as do *more* than half of all second marriages. I find such statistics truly sad because they reflect millions of shattered dreams.

I often wonder how well people know each other before they make a commitment. What do they know about each other's religion? Their politics? Views on raising children? Possible relocation plans? Housework? Shared interests? Sexual attitudes? Family relationships? Money? Pets? Goals? ...all those things and more!

Some people think, "Why worry? Love conquers all." They believe that if the relationship is a good one, these subjects will just fall into place, and everything will be wonderful.

...I don't think so.

Today, it's more important than ever to know *everything* you can about a potential partner. Getting to know someone sounds so simple. But it isn't. It's downright difficult and sometimes nearly impossible! In the early stages of a relationship, you may put your best foot forward so far you trip over it!

As you slowly learn more about each other, you discover each other's qualities — good and not so good. Sometimes even after years of togetherness, you may not know your partner's thoughts on some issues; you may mistake his or her silence as agreement with you.

This book may help you and your partner to communicate better.

HOW TO USE THIS BOOK

First of all, keep in mind it is not necessary to divulge every aspect of yourself to another person. However, there are some *important* issues you may wish to bring up with your partner, and this book will help you do that.

Review the Table of Contents before you start. You may wish to first complete only those areas that are most important to you and then complete the others at a later time. You will find some silly subjects along with the serious.

After identifying which topics you wish to complete, have your partner read, "Why You Need This Book" section as well as this "How To Use This Book" section.

You can then respond to the statements in one of two ways:

♥ First record *your* answers on a separate sheet of paper. Have your partner do the same on another piece of paper. Then compare answers and discuss your selected issues. (*This is your only option if this book is a library copy.*)

OR

♥ Sit down with your partner to read and answer each question together. Discuss the issues as you answer the questions or keep track of those issues you wish to discuss later.

As you complete the questionnaire, keep in mind **there are no correct answers**. This is an *opinion* questionnaire. I may not agree with your opinion. Your partner may not agree. Professionals may roll their eyes. The rest of the world may think you're crazy. Don't worry about what anyone else thinks! This is **your** opportunity to express what **you** think. Also, don't look for hidden meanings in the statements; they are pretty straightforward.

Answer the questions honestly, not how you think your partner *wants* you to answer them or how you think you *should* answer them. Each question is a statement, and you simply indicate whether or not you *agree* or *disagree* with the statement, and to what degree (Strongly disagree, Disagree, Agree, or Strongly agree).

You'll find another important choice called, "Let's discuss." Many issues are not black and white, and the statement may not offer enough information for you or your partner to decide if you agree or disagree with it. By marking, "Let's discuss," you open the door to further discussion. Selecting this option should be your last choice; use it only when none of the other answers are suitable.

You are free, of course, to discuss any statement, even one in which you feel strongly about and marked "Strongly agree" or "Strongly disagree." You may want to circle the statement so that you can refer to it later for further discussion.

As you answer these questions, remember your goal is *not* to match your partner's answers as closely as possible. If you are both honest in answering the questions, a great many of your answers will not match.

When your partner has completed the questionnaire, it is your turn to indicate if you agree or disagree with the statements. When you are finished, compare your answers. *Expect* that your partner's answers will be different from yours. Humans are snowflakes; no two are alike, and that is what makes life so interesting.

When you compare your answers, you can identify those areas in which you are compatible as well as incompatible. You may be surprised at each other's answers. You may discover issues that you never previously discussed. If you have *many* differences, select those that are most important to you and discuss them.

Be honest as you answer these questions. If you are not honest, you may as well not bother completing the exercise. If you are absolutely uncomfortable answering a question, select the "Let's discuss" option.

If you've been given this book by your partner — congratulations! You are a fortunate person because someone cares *very much* what you think about the world.

Now, sharpen your pencil, and if this is a library copy, find some paper to use for your answers instead of writing them in the book. Settle yourself into a quiet place where you can concentrate on reading and understanding each of the statements.

And as you answer these questions, remember — **honesty is the best policy**.

I. THE BASICS: BELIEFS, PREFERENCES, HABITS, AND HEALTH

If you read the Table of Contents, you know this chapter is the longest of the three chapters.   It covers a variety of topics, including: politics, gun control, education, sex, romance, smoking, tolerance of others, holiday expectations, pet preferences, and your ideal home.

Some of these topics you may have already discussed with your partner; others may never have come up in conversation.   Once again, I remind you: don't try to guess your partner's responses to these statements.   When you read the statement, decide if YOU agree or disagree; that is the purpose of this activity.   Be sure to read each statement carefully.

A.   General Beliefs

Basic Philosophies

For many people, religion is an important element in their lives. For others, it is insignificant. What about you? How does religion affect your life? In this section, you will identify your thoughts on the subject.

9

Basic Philosophies

DIRECTIONS: **IF you are a male,** place a check mark next to the response that most closely matches how much you agree or disagree with each statement. Select "Let's discuss" *only* if you believe the other answers are not appropriate. Place the check mark in the row opposite the "M," which stands for "male." **IF you are a female,** follow the same directions, except place your check mark on the row marked "F" for "female."

1.   I will truthfully answer the questions in this book.

M: ___a. Yes ___ b. No ___c. Let's discuss
F: ___a. Yes ___ b. No ___c. Let's discuss

2.   I believe that God is the supreme being who rules all things.

M: ___a. Strongly agree ___ b. Agree ___c. Disagree ___d. Strongly disagree ___e. Let's discuss
F: ___a. Strongly agree ___ b. Agree ___c. Disagree ___d. Strongly disagree ___e. Let's discuss

3.   I attend church on a regular basis.

M: ___a. Strongly agree ___ b. Agree ___c. Disagree ___d. Strongly disagree ___e. Let's discuss
F: ___a. Strongly agree ___ b. Agree ___c. Disagree ___d. Strongly disagree ___e. Let's discuss

4.   Religion is important to me.

M: ___a. Strongly agree ___ b. Agree ___c. Disagree ___d. Strongly disagree ___e. Let's discuss
F: ___a. Strongly agree ___ b. Agree ___c. Disagree ___d. Strongly disagree ___e. Let's discuss

5.   I would expect that anyone I married would convert to my religion if he/she were a member of a different faith.

M: ___a. Strongly agree ___ b. Agree ___c. Disagree ___d. Strongly disagree ___e. Let's discuss
F: ___a. Strongly agree ___ b. Agree ___c. Disagree ___d. Strongly disagree ___e. Let's discuss

6.   I would not expect anyone I married to convert to my religion, but I would be pleased.

M: ___a. Strongly agree ___ b. Agree ___c. Disagree ___d. Strongly disagree ___e. Let's discuss
F: ___a. Strongly agree ___ b. Agree ___c. Disagree ___d. Strongly disagree ___e. Let's discuss

7.   I would not associate with an atheist or agnostic.

M: ___a. Strongly agree ___ b. Agree ___c. Disagree ___d. Strongly disagree ___e. Let's discuss
F: ___a. Strongly agree ___ b. Agree ___c. Disagree ___d. Strongly disagree ___e. Let's discuss

8. **If I found a friend of mine was an atheist, I would try to convert my friend.**

M: ___a. Strongly agree ___ b. Agree ___c. Disagree ___d. Strongly disagree ___e. Let's discuss
F: ___a. Strongly agree ___ b. Agree ___c. Disagree ___d. Strongly disagree ___e. Let's discuss

9. **People who believe in a religion other than my own are to be pitied.**

M: ___a. Strongly agree ___ b. Agree ___c. Disagree ___d. Strongly disagree ___e. Let's discuss
F: ___a. Strongly agree ___ b. Agree ___c. Disagree ___d. Strongly disagree ___e. Let's discuss

10. **I believe my religion is the only true religion.**

M: ___a. Strongly agree ___ b. Agree ___c. Disagree ___d. Strongly disagree ___e. Let's discuss
F: ___a. Strongly agree ___ b. Agree ___c. Disagree ___d. Strongly disagree ___e. Let's discuss

11. **It is my responsibility to share the word of God.**

M: ___a. Strongly agree ___ b. Agree ___c. Disagree ___d. Strongly disagree ___e. Let's discuss
F: ___a. Strongly agree ___ b. Agree ___c. Disagree ___d. Strongly disagree ___e. Let's discuss

12. **I don't believe one religion is necessarily right or wrong; everyone is entitled to an opinion.**

M: ___a. Strongly agree ___ b. Agree ___c. Disagree ___d. Strongly disagree ___e. Let's discuss
F: ___a. Strongly agree ___ b. Agree ___c. Disagree ___d. Strongly disagree ___e. Let's discuss

13. **People who try to convert me to their religion drive me crazy.**

M: ___a. Strongly agree ___ b. Agree ___c. Disagree ___d. Strongly disagree ___e. Let's discuss
F: ___a. Strongly agree ___ b. Agree ___c. Disagree ___d. Strongly disagree ___e. Let's discuss

14. **I enjoy watching religious programs on TV.**

M: ___a. Strongly agree ___ b. Agree ___c. Disagree ___d. Strongly disagree ___e. Let's discuss
F: ___a. Strongly agree ___ b. Agree ___c. Disagree ___d. Strongly disagree ___e. Let's discuss

15. **If I had children, I would want to bring them up in my religion.**

M: ___a. Strongly agree ___ b. Agree ___c. Disagree ___d. Strongly disagree ___e. Let's discuss
F: ___a. Strongly agree ___ b. Agree ___c. Disagree ___d. Strongly disagree ___e. Let's discuss

16. I enjoy discussing philosophical ideas.

M: ___a. Strongly agree ___ b. Agree ___c. Disagree ___d. Strongly disagree ___e. Let's discuss
F: ___a. Strongly agree ___ b. Agree ___c. Disagree ___d. Strongly disagree ___e. Let's discuss

17. I consider myself a spiritual person. (Note: You may wish to share with your partner *your* definition of "spiritual.")

M: ___a. Strongly agree ___ b. Agree ___c. Disagree ___d. Strongly disagree ___e. Let's discuss
F: ___a. Strongly agree ___ b. Agree ___c. Disagree ___d. Strongly disagree ___e. Let's discuss

18. It's okay to lie once in a while if it doesn't hurt anyone.

M: ___a. Strongly agree ___ b. Agree ___c. Disagree ___d. Strongly disagree ___e. Let's discuss
F: ___a. Strongly agree ___ b. Agree ___c. Disagree ___d. Strongly disagree ___e. Let's discuss

19. Most people cheat on their taxes.

M: ___a. Strongly agree ___ b. Agree ___c. Disagree ___d. Strongly disagree ___e. Let's discuss
F: ___a. Strongly agree ___ b. Agree ___c. Disagree ___d. Strongly disagree ___e. Let's discuss

20. It is nobody's business (including the government's) how much money I make.

M: ___a. Strongly agree ___ b. Agree ___c. Disagree ___d. Strongly disagree ___e. Let's discuss
F: ___a. Strongly agree ___ b. Agree ___c. Disagree ___d. Strongly disagree ___e. Let's discuss

21. It's okay to lie in order to avoid hurting someone's feelings.

M: ___a. Strongly agree ___ b. Agree ___c. Disagree ___d. Strongly disagree ___e. Let's discuss
F: ___a. Strongly agree ___ b. Agree ___c. Disagree ___d. Strongly disagree ___e. Let's discuss

22. It's okay to be dishonest with big companies because they make a lot of money off the little guy.

M: ___a. Strongly agree ___ b. Agree ___c. Disagree ___d. Strongly disagree ___e. Let's discuss
F: ___a. Strongly agree ___ b. Agree ___c. Disagree ___d. Strongly disagree ___e. Let's discuss

23.   It's okay to steal small items, such as pens, tape dispensers, and staplers from your employer.

M: ___a. Strongly agree   ___ b. Agree   ___c. Disagree   ___d. Strongly disagree   ___e. Let's discuss
F: ___a. Strongly agree   ___ b. Agree   ___c. Disagree   ___d. Strongly disagree   ___e. Let's discuss

24.   If I needed money to feed my family, I would do what I had to do to get it, even if it was against the law.

M: ___a. Strongly agree   ___ b. Agree   ___c. Disagree   ___d. Strongly disagree   ___e. Let's discuss
F: ___a. Strongly agree   ___ b. Agree   ___c. Disagree   ___d. Strongly disagree   ___e. Let's discuss

25.   Some people are just meant to be together; it is fact of life that you may meet that person while you are married to someone else.

M: ___a. Strongly agree   ___ b. Agree   ___c. Disagree   ___d. Strongly disagree   ___e. Let's discuss
F: ___a. Strongly agree   ___ b. Agree   ___c. Disagree   ___d. Strongly disagree   ___e. Let's discuss

26.   Falling in love with someone else while you are married is not as bad as just having a purely sexual extramarital affair.

M: ___a. Strongly agree   ___ b. Agree   ___c. Disagree   ___d. Strongly disagree   ___e. Let's discuss
F: ___a. Strongly agree   ___ b. Agree   ___c. Disagree   ___d. Strongly disagree   ___e. Let's discuss

27.   If my spouse cheated on me, I would probably forgive my spouse. (Note: You may wish to define with your partner *your* exact definition of "cheating")

M: ___a. Strongly agree   ___ b. Agree   ___c. Disagree   ___d. Strongly disagree   ___e. Let's discuss
F: ___a. Strongly agree   ___ b. Agree   ___c. Disagree   ___d. Strongly disagree   ___e. Let's discuss

Politics

Do you believe that successful relationships are based on shared values, including shared political beliefs? In this section, you'll find out if your political views differ.

DIRECTIONS: **IF you are a male,** place your check mark next to the response that most closely matches how much you agree or disagree with each statement. Select "Let's discuss" *only* if you believe the other answers are not appropriate. Place your check mark in the row opposite the "M," which stands for "male." **IF you are a female,** follow the same directions, except place your check mark on the row marked "F" for "female."

28.   I vote.

M: ___a. Yes ___ b. No ___c. Let's discuss
F: ___a. Yes ___ b. No ___c. Let's discuss

29.   It doesn't matter whether or not I vote.

M: ___a. Strongly agree ___ b. Agree ___c. Disagree ___d. Strongly disagree ___e. Let's discuss
F: ___a. Strongly agree ___ b. Agree ___c. Disagree ___d. Strongly disagree ___e. Let's discuss

30.   It bothers me if I miss an opportunity to vote in a local or national election.

M: ___a. Strongly agree ___ b. Agree ___c. Disagree ___d. Strongly disagree ___e. Let's discuss
F: ___a. Strongly agree ___ b. Agree ___c. Disagree ___d. Strongly disagree ___e. Let's discuss

31.   If I had to choose one party that most closely matches my beliefs, it would be the Republican party.

M: ___a. Strongly agree ___ b. Agree ___c. Disagree ___d. Strongly disagree ___e. Let's discuss
F: ___a. Strongly agree ___ b. Agree ___c. Disagree ___d. Strongly disagree ___e. Let's discuss

14

32. **If I had to choose one party that most closely matches my beliefs, it would be the Democratic party.**

M: ___a. Strongly agree ___ b. Agree ___c. Disagree ___d. Strongly disagree ___e. Let's discuss
F: ___a. Strongly agree ___ b. Agree ___c. Disagree ___d. Strongly disagree ___e. Let's discuss

33. **I always vote along party lines.**

M: ___a. Strongly agree ___ b. Agree ___c. Disagree ___d. Strongly disagree ___e. Let's discuss
F: ___a. Strongly agree ___ b. Agree ___c. Disagree ___d. Strongly disagree ___e. Let's discuss

34. **When I vote, I evaluate the candidate and don't pay much attention to specific party affiliations.**

M: ___a. Strongly agree ___ b. Agree ___c. Disagree ___d. Strongly disagree ___e. Let's discuss
F: ___a. Strongly agree ___ b. Agree ___c. Disagree ___d. Strongly disagree ___e. Let's discuss

35. **As far as political views, I consider myself a moderate.**

M: ___a. Strongly agree ___ b. Agree ___c. Disagree ___d. Strongly disagree ___e. Let's discuss
F: ___a. Strongly agree ___ b. Agree ___c. Disagree ___d. Strongly disagree ___e. Let's discuss

36. **I consider myself liberal.**

M: ___a. Strongly agree ___ b. Agree ___c. Disagree ___d. Strongly disagree ___e. Let's discuss
F: ___a. Strongly agree ___ b. Agree ___c. Disagree ___d. Strongly disagree ___e. Let's discuss

37. **I consider myself conservative.**

M: ___a. Strongly agree ___ b. Agree ___c. Disagree ___d. Strongly disagree ___e. Let's discuss
F: ___a. Strongly agree ___ b. Agree ___c. Disagree ___d. Strongly disagree ___e. Let's discuss

38. **I believe it is important for my partner to share my political views.**

M: ___a. Strongly agree ___ b. Agree ___c. Disagree ___d. Strongly disagree ___e. Let's discuss
F: ___a. Strongly agree ___ b. Agree ___c. Disagree ___d. Strongly disagree ___e. Let's discuss

39. **I would like someday to become more knowledgeable about politics.**

M: ___a. Strongly agree ___ b. Agree ___c. Disagree ___d. Strongly disagree ___e. Let's discuss
F: ___a. Strongly agree ___ b. Agree ___c. Disagree ___d. Strongly disagree ___e. Let's discuss

40. I would like someday to become more involved in politics.

M: ___a. Strongly agree ___ b. Agree ___c. Disagree ___d. Strongly disagree ___e. Let's discuss
F: ___a. Strongly agree ___ b. Agree ___c. Disagree ___d. Strongly disagree ___e. Let's discuss

Guns

Does the thought of a gun in your house scare you to death? Or do you feel safer knowing you can use a gun to scare off an intruder? If you don't own a gun, can you live with someone who believes a gun is one of life's necessities? If you own a gun and your partner is uncomfortable with a gun in the house, are you willing to get rid of the gun?

DIRECTIONS: **IF you are a male,** place your check mark next to the response that most closely matches how much you agree or disagree with each statement. Select "Let's discuss" *only* if you believe the other answers are not appropriate. Place your checkmark in the row opposite the "M," which stands for "male." **IF you are a female,** follow the same directions, except place your checkmark on the row marked "F" for "female."

41. I own a gun.

M: ___a. Yes ___ b. No ___c. Let's discuss
F: ___a. Yes ___ b. No ___c. Let's discuss

42. I think it's important that all citizens be armed.

M: ___a. Strongly agree ___ b. Agree ___c. Disagree ___d. Strongly disagree ___e. Let's discuss
F: ___a. Strongly agree ___ b. Agree ___c. Disagree ___d. Strongly disagree ___e. Let's discuss

43. The main reason violence is a problem in our society is because too many people have guns.

M: ___a. Strongly agree ___ b. Agree ___c. Disagree ___d. Strongly disagree ___e. Let's discuss
F: ___a. Strongly agree ___ b. Agree ___c. Disagree ___d. Strongly disagree ___e. Let's discuss

44. Gun control laws should be stricter.

M: ___a. Strongly agree ___ b. Agree ___c. Disagree ___d. Strongly disagree ___e. Let's discuss
F: ___a. Strongly agree ___ b. Agree ___c. Disagree ___d. Strongly disagree ___e. Let's discuss

45. Toy guns should be banned.

M: ___a. Strongly agree ___ b. Agree ___c. Disagree ___d. Strongly disagree ___e. Let's discuss
F: ___a. Strongly agree ___ b. Agree ___c. Disagree ___d. Strongly disagree ___e. Let's discuss

46. I enjoy hunting.

M: ___a. Strongly agree ___ b. Agree ___c. Disagree ___d. Strongly disagree ___e. Let's discuss
F: ___a. Strongly agree ___ b. Agree ___c. Disagree ___d. Strongly disagree ___e. Let's discuss

Let me get this straight. You've been divorced three times in _this_ life, but you were happily married to a coal miner during the 1800's in your _previous_ life?"

Marital History

If you have been previously married, consider your marriage as a college-level course in human behavior. If, after healing from the hurt of a broken relationship, you are able to identify exactly what happened and why, and if you can apply this newfound knowledge to future relationships, you have passed the course with flying colors!

DIRECTIONS: **IF you are a male,** place your check mark next to the response that most closely matches how much you agree or disagree with each statement. Select "Let's discuss" *only* if you believe the other answers are not appropriate. Place your checkmark in the row opposite the "M," which stands for "male." **IF you are a female,** follow the same directions, except place your checkmark on the row marked "F" for "female."

47.   I have been married once before.

M:　　＿＿a. Yes ＿＿ b. No ＿＿c. Let's discuss
F:　　＿＿a. Yes ＿＿ b. No ＿＿c. Let's discuss

NOTE:　　*Answer the following five questions only if you have been previously married.*

48.   I have been married two or more times.

M:　　＿＿a. Yes ＿＿ b. No ＿＿c. Let's discuss
F:　　＿＿a. Yes ＿＿ b. No ＿＿c. Let's discuss

49.   I am still *legally* married.

M:　　＿＿a. Yes ＿＿ b. No ＿＿c. Let's discuss
F:　　＿＿a. Yes ＿＿ b. No ＿＿c. Let's discuss

50. **I am a somewhat changed person as a result of my previous marriage(s) and divorce(s).**

M: ___a. Strongly agree ___ b. Agree ___c. Disagree ___d. Strongly disagree ___e. Let's discuss
F: ___a. Strongly agree ___ b. Agree ___c. Disagree ___d. Strongly disagree ___e. Let's discuss

51. **It was through no fault of my own that my previous marriage(s) ended.**

M: ___a. Strongly agree ___ b. Agree ___c. Disagree ___d. Strongly disagree ___e. Let's discuss
F: ___a. Strongly agree ___ b. Agree ___c. Disagree ___d. Strongly disagree ___e. Let's discuss

52. **I would do some things differently if I were to remarry.**

M: ___a. Strongly agree ___ b. Agree ___c. Disagree ___d. Strongly disagree ___e. Let's discuss
F: ___a. Strongly agree ___ b. Agree ___c. Disagree ___d. Strongly disagree ___e. Let's discuss

---

Education

The purpose of this section is not to find out where you went to school and for how long. That information, I assume, was covered early in your relationship. Instead, this section helps identify your attitude about learning more about the world around you.

DIRECTIONS: **IF you are a male,** place your check mark next to the response that most closely matches how much you agree or disagree with each statement. Select "Let's discuss" *only* if you believe the other answers are not appropriate. Place your checkmark in the row opposite the "M," which stands for "male." **IF you are a female,** follow the same directions, except place your checkmark on the row marked "F" for "female."

53. **I never read the newspaper because it's nothing but bad news anyway.**

M: ___a. Yes ___ b. No ___c. Let's discuss
F: ___a. Yes ___ b. No ___c. Let's discuss

20

54. I try to read the newspaper every day.

M: ___a. Yes ___ b. No ___c. Let's discuss
F: ___a. Yes ___ b. No ___c. Let's discuss

55. I am rarely interested in anything that is on the TV news.

M: ___a. Yes ___ b. No ___c. Let's discuss
F: ___a. Yes ___ b. No ___c. Let's discuss

56. I listen to the radio to hear about local and world events.

M: ___a. Yes ___ b. No ___c. Let's discuss
F: ___a. Yes ___ b. No ___c. Let's discuss

57. I often read books.

M: ___a. Yes ___ b. No ___c. Let's discuss
F: ___a. Yes ___ b. No ___c. Let's discuss

58. I often read magazines.

M: ___a. Yes ___ b. No ___c. Let's discuss
F: ___a. Yes ___ b. No ___c. Let's discuss

59. I hate to read.

M: ___a. Yes ___ b. No ___c. Let's discuss
F: ___a. Yes ___ b. No ___c. Let's discuss

60. Continuing education (gaining knowledge about the world), for people of any age, is important.

M: ___a. Strongly agree ___ b. Agree ___c. Disagree ___d. Strongly disagree ___e. Let's discuss
F: ___a. Strongly agree ___ b. Agree ___c. Disagree ___d. Strongly disagree ___e. Let's discuss

61. A college education is very important.

M: ___a. Strongly agree ___ b. Agree ___c. Disagree ___d. Strongly disagree ___e. Let's discuss
F: ___a. Strongly agree ___ b. Agree ___c. Disagree ___d. Strongly disagree ___e. Let's discuss

62. I am uncomfortable around people who are not educated.

M: ___a. Strongly agree ___ b. Agree ___c. Disagree ___d. Strongly disagree ___e. Let's discuss
F: ___a. Strongly agree ___ b. Agree ___c. Disagree ___d. Strongly disagree ___e. Let's discuss

63. An advanced degree is very important.

M: ___a. Strongly agree ___ b. Agree ___c. Disagree ___d. Strongly disagree ___e. Let's discuss
F: ___a. Strongly agree ___ b. Agree ___c. Disagree ___d. Strongly disagree ___e. Let's discuss

64. Educated people are snobs.

M: ___a. Strongly agree ___ b. Agree ___c. Disagree ___d. Strongly disagree ___e. Let's discuss
F: ___a. Strongly agree ___ b. Agree ___c. Disagree ___d. Strongly disagree ___e. Let's discuss

65. If I had children, I would insist that they completed a college education.

M: ___a. Strongly agree ___ b. Agree ___c. Disagree ___d. Strongly disagree ___e. Let's discuss
F: ___a. Strongly agree ___ b. Agree ___c. Disagree ___d. Strongly disagree ___e. Let's discuss

Hey, I ain't gotta read no books. I watch cable, like, 14 hours a day, man.

C.   Other People

Race

Race relations is not a common topic between two people in love. Sometimes a person's feelings about race may not surface for years. Here is your opportunity to find out your partner's beliefs on the subject.

DIRECTIONS: **IF you are a male,** place your check mark next to the response that most closely matches how much you agree or disagree with each statement. Select "Let's discuss" *only* if you believe the other answers are not appropriate. Place your checkmark in the row opposite the "M," which stands for "male."   **IF you are a female,** follow the same directions, except place your checkmark on the row marked "F" for "female."

66.   I would not live in a racially mixed neighborhood.

M: ___a. Yes ___ b. No ___c. Let's discuss
F: ___a. Yes ___ b. No ___c. Let's discuss

67.   I would not want my child to *marry* a person of a race different from my own.

M: ___a. Strongly agree ___ b. Agree ___c. Disagree ___d. Strongly disagree ___e. Let's discuss
F: ___a. Strongly agree ___ b. Agree ___c. Disagree ___d. Strongly disagree ___e. Let's discuss

68.   I would not want my child to *date* a person of a race different from my own.

M: ___a. Strongly agree ___ b. Agree ___c. Disagree ___d. Strongly disagree ___e. Let's discuss
F: ___a. Strongly agree ___ b. Agree ___c. Disagree ___d. Strongly disagree ___e. Let's discuss

Race

69. I believe the races should be separate.

M: ___a. Strongly agree ___ b. Agree ___c. Disagree ___d. Strongly disagree ___e. Let's discuss
F: ___a. Strongly agree ___ b. Agree ___c. Disagree ___d. Strongly disagree ___e. Let's discuss

70. I prefer to live in a racially mixed neighborhood.

M: ___a. Strongly agree ___ b. Agree ___c. Disagree ___d. Strongly disagree ___e. Let's discuss
F: ___a. Strongly agree ___ b. Agree ___c. Disagree ___d. Strongly disagree ___e. Let's discuss

71. I would not hire a person of another race if given the opportunity, even if the person were the best qualified for the job.

M: ___a. Strongly agree ___ b. Agree ___c. Disagree ___d. Strongly disagree ___e. Let's discuss
F: ___a. Strongly agree ___ b. Agree ___c. Disagree ___d. Strongly disagree ___e. Let's discuss

72. If I were an apartment owner, I would not rent an apartment to a person of a race different from my own.

M: ___a. Strongly agree ___ b. Agree ___c. Disagree ___d. Strongly disagree ___e. Let's discuss
F: ___a. Strongly agree ___ b. Agree ___c. Disagree ___d. Strongly disagree ___e. Let's discuss

73. There is nothing wrong with interracial marriage.

M: ___a. Strongly agree ___ b. Agree ___c. Disagree ___d. Strongly disagree ___e. Let's discuss
F: ___a. Strongly agree ___ b. Agree ___c. Disagree ___d. Strongly disagree ___e. Let's discuss

74. Although I know a *few* good people of a race different from mine, most people who are not of my race are not to be trusted.

M: ___a. Strongly agree ___ b. Agree ___c. Disagree ___d. Strongly disagree ___e. Let's discuss
F: ___a. Strongly agree ___ b. Agree ___c. Disagree ___d. Strongly disagree ___e. Let's discuss

75. I believe all people are equal and should be treated the same.

M: ___a. Strongly agree ___ b. Agree ___c. Disagree ___d. Strongly disagree ___e. Let's discuss
F: ___a. Strongly agree ___ b. Agree ___c. Disagree ___d. Strongly disagree ___e. Let's discuss

Race

76. Character, not the color of a person's skin, is what matters.

M: ___a. Strongly agree ___ b. Agree ___c. Disagree ___d. Strongly disagree ___e. Let's discuss
F: ___a. Strongly agree ___ b. Agree ___c. Disagree ___d. Strongly disagree ___e. Let's discuss

77. I have friends of a race different from my own.

M: ___a. Strongly agree ___ b. Agree ___c. Disagree ___d. Strongly disagree ___e. Let's discuss
F: ___a. Strongly agree ___ b. Agree ___c. Disagree ___d. Strongly disagree ___e. Let's discuss

78. If given the opportunity, I would have no objection to hiring someone of a race different from my own.

M: ___a. Strongly agree ___ b. Agree ___c. Disagree ___d. Strongly disagree ___e. Let's discuss
F: ___a. Strongly agree ___ b. Agree ___c. Disagree ___d. Strongly disagree ___e. Let's discuss

79. I would have no objection to working for someone of a race different from my own.

M: ___a. Strongly agree ___ b. Agree ___c. Disagree ___d. Strongly disagree ___e. Let's discuss
F: ___a. Strongly agree ___ b. Agree ___c. Disagree ___d. Strongly disagree ___e. Let's discuss

Homosexuality

Do you or your partner judge people by their sexual orientation? Do your religious beliefs reinforce your ideas? Do you believe all people should be judged by their character? If you have gay/lesbian friends or relatives, how does your partner feel about them?

DIRECTIONS: **IF you are a male,** place your check mark next to the response that most closely matches how much you agree or disagree with each statement. Select "Let's discuss" *only* if you believe the other answers are not appropriate. Place your check mark in the row opposite the "M," which stands for "male." **IF you are a female**, follow the same directions, except place your check mark on the row marked "F" for "female."

80. **I am angered by people who are intolerant of gay and lesbian people.**

M: ___a. Strongly agree ___ b. Agree ___c. Disagree ___d. Strongly disagree ___e. Let's discuss
F: ___a. Strongly agree ___ b. Agree ___c. Disagree ___d. Strongly disagree ___e. Let's discuss

81. **I am uncomfortable around gay or lesbian people.**

M: ___a. Strongly agree ___ b. Agree ___c. Disagree ___d. Strongly disagree ___e. Let's discuss
F: ___a. Strongly agree ___ b. Agree ___c. Disagree ___d. Strongly disagree ___e. Let's discuss

82. **As far as gay or lesbian people are concerned, I say, "Live and let live."**

M: ___a. Strongly agree ___ b. Agree ___c. Disagree ___d. Strongly disagree ___e. Let's discuss
F: ___a. Strongly agree ___ b. Agree ___c. Disagree ___d. Strongly disagree ___e. Let's discuss

83. **I would not hire a gay or lesbian person.**

M: ___a. Strongly agree ___ b. Agree ___c. Disagree ___d. Strongly disagree ___e. Let's discuss
F: ___a. Strongly agree ___ b. Agree ___c. Disagree ___d. Strongly disagree ___e. Let's discuss

84. **People who hate gay and/or lesbian people do so out of ignorance and irrational fear.**

M: ___a. Strongly agree ___ b. Agree ___c. Disagree ___d. Strongly disagree ___e. Let's discuss
F: ___a. Strongly agree ___ b. Agree ___c. Disagree ___d. Strongly disagree ___e. Let's discuss

85. **Because of my religious convictions, I believe the sexual behavior of gay and lesbian people is unacceptable.**

M: ___a. Strongly agree ___ b. Agree ___c. Disagree ___d. Strongly disagree ___e. Let's discuss
F: ___a. Strongly agree ___ b. Agree ___c. Disagree ___d. Strongly disagree ___e. Let's discuss

86. **If I found out that a friend of mine was gay, I would continue the friendship.**

M: ___a. Strongly agree ___ b. Agree ___c. Disagree ___d. Strongly disagree ___e. Let's discuss
F: ___a. Strongly agree ___ b. Agree ___c. Disagree ___d. Strongly disagree ___e. Let's discuss

87. If my partner had a gay or lesbian friend or relative, I would avoid that person.

M: ___a. Strongly agree ___ b. Agree ___c. Disagree ___d. Strongly disagree ___e. Let's discuss
F: ___a. Strongly agree ___ b. Agree ___c. Disagree ___d. Strongly disagree ___e. Let's discuss

88. People should be judged on character and not on sexual orientation.

M: ___a. Strongly agree ___ b. Agree ___c. Disagree ___d. Strongly disagree ___e. Let's discuss
F: ___a. Strongly agree ___ b. Agree ___c. Disagree ___d. Strongly disagree ___e. Let's discuss

Body Weight

As your partner's lover, you hold an incredible amount of power to bolster your partner's self-esteem. Use this power wisely. Take every opportunity to admire your partner, regardless of his or her weight. Smile. Compliment. *Enjoy* each other! Life's too short to do otherwise.

DIRECTIONS: **IF you are a male,** place your check mark next to the response that most closely matches how much you agree or disagree with each statement. Select "Let's discuss" *only* if you believe the other answers are not appropriate. Place your check mark in the row opposite the "M," which stands for "male." **IF you are a female,** follow the same directions, except place your check mark on the row marked "F" for "female."

89. People are obsessed with their weight these days, and I think whether or not a person is overweight is not important, just as long as they are healthy.

M: ___a. Strongly agree ___ b. Agree ___c. Disagree ___d. Strongly disagree ___e. Let's discuss
F: ___a. Strongly agree ___ b. Agree ___c. Disagree ___d. Strongly disagree ___e. Let's discuss

90. Overweight people are unattractive.

M: ___a. Strongly agree ___ b. Agree ___c. Disagree ___d. Strongly disagree ___e. Let's discuss
F: ___a. Strongly agree ___ b. Agree ___c. Disagree ___d. Strongly disagree ___e. Let's discuss

91. **I become angry when I hear people tell jokes ridiculing overweight people.**

M: ___a. Strongly agree ___ b. Agree ___c. Disagree ___d. Strongly disagree ___e. Let's discuss
F: ___a. Strongly agree ___ b. Agree ___c. Disagree ___d. Strongly disagree ___e. Let's discuss

92. **Most overweight people don't try hard enough to lose weight.**

M: ___a. Strongly agree ___ b. Agree ___c. Disagree ___d. Strongly disagree ___e. Let's discuss
F: ___a. Strongly agree ___ b. Agree ___c. Disagree ___d. Strongly disagree ___e. Let's discuss

93. **If my partner put on weight during our relationship, that would be reason enough for me to end the relationship.**

M: ___a. Strongly agree ___ b. Agree ___c. Disagree ___d. Strongly disagree ___e. Let's discuss
F: ___a. Strongly agree ___ b. Agree ___c. Disagree ___d. Strongly disagree ___e. Let's discuss

94. **I regularly exercise to keep myself in shape, and I expect my partner to do the same.**

M: ___a. Strongly agree ___ b. Agree ___c. Disagree ___d. Strongly disagree ___e. Let's discuss
F: ___a. Strongly agree ___ b. Agree ___c. Disagree ___d. Strongly disagree ___e. Let's discuss

95. **I would be embarrassed to be seen in public with an overweight person.**

M: ___a. Strongly agree ___ b. Agree ___c. Disagree ___d. Strongly disagree ___e. Let's discuss
F: ___a. Strongly agree ___ b. Agree ___c. Disagree ___d. Strongly disagree ___e. Let's discuss

96. **It is more difficult for women to lose weight than it is for men.**

M: ___a. Strongly agree ___ b. Agree ___c. Disagree ___d. Strongly disagree ___e. Let's discuss
F: ___a. Strongly agree ___ b. Agree ___c. Disagree ___d. Strongly disagree ___e. Let's discuss

97. **I prefer a partner with some "meat" on his or her bones.**

M: ___a. Strongly agree ___ b. Agree ___c. Disagree ___d. Strongly disagree ___e. Let's discuss
F: ___a. Strongly agree ___ b. Agree ___c. Disagree ___d. Strongly disagree ___e. Let's discuss

Friends

Some couples are each other's best friends and would never have it any other way. Other couples have their own separate friends. What about you? Is your partner your best friend?

DIRECTIONS: **IF you are a male,** place your check mark next to the response that most closely matches how much you agree or disagree with each statement. Select "Let's discuss" *only* if you believe the other answers are not appropriate. Place your checkmark in the row opposite the "M," which stands for "male." **IF you are a female,** follow the same directions, except place your checkmark on the row marked "F" for "female."

98. A husband and wife should be each other's best friend.

M: ___ a. Strongly agree ___ b. Agree ___ c. Disagree ___ d. Strongly disagree ___ e. Let's discuss
F: ___ a. Strongly agree ___ b. Agree ___ c. Disagree ___ d. Strongly disagree ___ e. Let's discuss

99. It is healthy if a person has many different types of people in his or her life.

M: ___ a. Strongly agree ___ b. Agree ___ c. Disagree ___ d. Strongly disagree ___ e. Let's discuss
F: ___ a. Strongly agree ___ b. Agree ___ c. Disagree ___ d. Strongly disagree ___ e. Let's discuss

100. In a good marriage, neither partner needs anyone else but each other.

M: ___ a. Strongly agree ___ b. Agree ___ c. Disagree ___ d. Strongly disagree ___ e. Let's discuss
F: ___ a. Strongly agree ___ b. Agree ___ c. Disagree ___ d. Strongly disagree ___ e. Let's discuss

101. I am sometimes jealous of the time my partner spends with his or her friends.

M: ___ a. Strongly agree ___ b. Agree ___ c. Disagree ___ d. Strongly disagree ___ e. Let's discuss
F: ___ a. Strongly agree ___ b. Agree ___ c. Disagree ___ d. Strongly disagree ___ e. Let's discuss

102. When two people marry, they should not go out with their single friends as they did before they married.

M: ___a. Strongly agree ___ b. Agree ___c. Disagree ___d. Strongly disagree ___e. Let's discuss
F: ___a. Strongly agree ___ b. Agree ___c. Disagree ___d. Strongly disagree ___e. Let's discuss

103. It is possible for a person to have a member of the opposite sex as a very good friend and not be lovers.

M: ___a. Strongly agree ___ b. Agree ___c. Disagree ___d. Strongly disagree ___e. Let's discuss
F: ___a. Strongly agree ___ b. Agree ___c. Disagree ___d. Strongly disagree ___e. Let's discuss

104. Once a person is married, that person should not maintain daily contact with his or her parents.

M: ___a. Strongly agree ___ b. Agree ___c. Disagree ___d. Strongly disagree ___e. Let's discuss
F: ___a. Strongly agree ___ b. Agree ___c. Disagree ___d. Strongly disagree ___e. Let's discuss

105. I enjoy going out with my friends on a regular basis, and I have no plans to discontinue doing that even if I am in a romantic relationship.

M: ___a. Strongly agree ___ b. Agree ___c. Disagree ___d. Strongly disagree ___e. Let's discuss
F: ___a. Strongly agree ___ b. Agree ___c. Disagree ___d. Strongly disagree ___e. Let's discuss

106. If I don't like my partner's friends, I don't have to associate with them.

M: ___a. Strongly agree ___ b. Agree ___c. Disagree ___d. Strongly disagree ___e. Let's discuss
F: ___a. Strongly agree ___ b. Agree ___c. Disagree ___d. Strongly disagree ___e. Let's discuss

107. I like to joke about my partner's shortcomings.

M: ___a. Strongly agree ___ b. Agree ___c. Disagree ___d. Strongly disagree ___e. Let's discuss
F: ___a. Strongly agree ___ b. Agree ___c. Disagree ___d. Strongly disagree ___e. Let's discuss

108. You should never insult your partner in front of other people.

M: ___a. Strongly agree ___ b. Agree ___c. Disagree ___d. Strongly disagree ___e. Let's discuss
F: ___a. Strongly agree ___ b. Agree ___c. Disagree ___d. Strongly disagree ___e. Let's discuss

109. **It may not be a good idea to discuss my marital problems with my friends because they may hold a grudge against my partner once the problems are resolved.**

M: ___a. Strongly agree ___b. Agree ___c. Disagree ___d. Strongly disagree ___e. Let's discuss
F: ___a. Strongly agree ___b. Agree ___c. Disagree ___d. Strongly disagree ___e. Let's discuss

110. **I get angry when my partner does not share his or her feelings with me.**

M: ___a. Strongly agree ___b. Agree ___c. Disagree ___d. Strongly disagree ___e. Let's discuss
F: ___a. Strongly agree ___b. Agree ___c. Disagree ___d. Strongly disagree ___e. Let's discuss

How dare you treat Susan like that, you lousy rotten creep! She told me all about it last week! You make me sick, you stupid jerk, you ....

We made up last night. We're engaged.

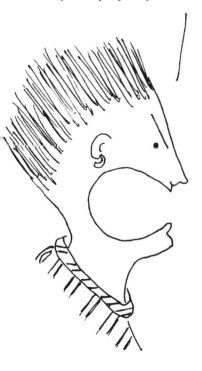

31

D. Basic Needs

These are the basics — food, clothing, and shelter. Do you love to eat but hate to cook? Perhaps your partner loves to cook. (Lucky you!) Maybe you both love to sample new foods and try new restaurants.

Are clothes important to you? Do you wear only the latest styles and expect your sweetie to do the same? Perhaps clothes are a non-issue. Maybe your partner, given the choice, would prefer not wearing any clothes at all!

Do you love decorating your home? Do you find satisfaction in creating beautiful gardens? More than a few relationships have failed because one partner placed a far greater value on house and home than did the other partner. There's nothing wrong with wanting to pursue other activities besides raking leaves or installing storm doors. But if you enjoy home maintenance, it may be helpful to find out if your partner shares your interest.

Food

Would you love to go out to eat every night of the week? Or do you prefer to stay home? Do you turn green at the thought of ethnic foods? Are you afraid to try anything that still has its eyeballs? Maybe you find American food dull and relish the idea of trying foods from around the world. Answer these questions and find out if you and your partner agree on this activity that takes up so much of our lives.

DIRECTIONS: **IF you are a male,** place your check mark next to the response that most closely matches how much you agree or disagree with each statement. Select "Let's discuss" *only* if you believe the other answers are not appropriate. Place your checkmark in the row opposite the "M," which stands for "male." **IF you are a female,** follow the same directions, except place your checkmark on the row marked "F" for "female."

111.   I expect my partner to be a good cook.

M: ___a. Strongly agree ___ b. Agree ___c. Disagree ___d. Strongly disagree ___e. Let's discuss
F: ___a. Strongly agree ___ b. Agree ___c. Disagree ___d. Strongly disagree ___e. Let's discuss

112.   I like to cook.

M: ___a. Strongly agree ___ b. Agree ___c. Disagree ___d. Strongly disagree ___e. Let's discuss
F: ___a. Strongly agree ___ b. Agree ___c. Disagree ___d. Strongly disagree ___e. Let's discuss

113.   I enjoy eating at home.

M: ___a. Strongly agree ___ b. Agree ___c. Disagree ___d. Strongly disagree ___e. Let's discuss
F: ___a. Strongly agree ___ b. Agree ___c. Disagree ___d. Strongly disagree ___e. Let's discuss

114.   I am uncomfortable eating in front of other people.

M: ___a. Strongly agree ___ b. Agree ___c. Disagree ___d. Strongly disagree ___e. Let's discuss
F: ___a. Strongly agree ___ b. Agree ___c. Disagree ___d. Strongly disagree ___e. Let's discuss

115.   It drives me crazy when people make a lot of noise (chomping, smacking lips, grunting) when they eat.

M: ___a. Strongly agree ___ b. Agree ___c. Disagree ___d. Strongly disagree ___e. Let's discuss
F: ___a. Strongly agree ___ b. Agree ___c. Disagree ___d. Strongly disagree ___e. Let's discuss

116.   I prefer a "meat and potato" type of a meal over anything else.

M: ___a. Strongly agree ___ b. Agree ___c. Disagree ___d. Strongly disagree ___e. Let's discuss
F: ___a. Strongly agree ___ b. Agree ___c. Disagree ___d. Strongly disagree ___e. Let's discuss

Food

117. I enjoy eating at restaurants.

M: ___a. Strongly agree ___ b. Agree ___c. Disagree ___d. Strongly disagree ___e. Let's discuss
F: ___a. Strongly agree ___ b. Agree ___c. Disagree ___d. Strongly disagree ___e. Let's discuss

118. I like trying ethnic foods (such as Chinese, Vietnamese, Korean, Greek, Indian, Mexican).

M: ___a. Strongly agree ___ b. Agree ___c. Disagree ___d. Strongly disagree ___e. Let's discuss
F: ___a. Strongly agree ___ b. Agree ___c. Disagree ___d. Strongly disagree ___e. Let's discuss

119. I am not fussy about what I eat.

M: ___a. Strongly agree ___ b. Agree ___c. Disagree ___d. Strongly disagree ___e. Let's discuss
F: ___a. Strongly agree ___ b. Agree ___c. Disagree ___d. Strongly disagree ___e. Let's discuss

Clothing

Do you think clothes reflect the wearer's personality? Are you put off by people who prefer to wear old, worn clothes when they can afford better ones? Do you enjoy wearing the latest fashions?

DIRECTIONS: **IF you are a male,** place your check mark next to the response that most closely matches how much you agree or disagree with each statement. Select "Let's discuss" *only* if you believe the other answers are not appropriate. Place your check mark in the row opposite the "M," which stands for "male." **IF you are a female,** follow the same directions, except place your check mark on the row marked "F" for "female."

120. I expect my partner to dress in up-to-date styles.

M: ___a. Strongly agree ___ b. Agree ___c. Disagree ___d. Strongly disagree ___e. Let's discuss
F: ___a. Strongly agree ___ b. Agree ___c. Disagree ___d. Strongly disagree ___e. Let's discuss

121. I would be embarrassed to be seen in public with my partner if my partner wore old clothes.

M: ___a. Strongly agree ___ b. Agree ___c. Disagree ___d. Strongly disagree ___e. Let's discuss
F: ___a. Strongly agree ___ b. Agree ___c. Disagree ___d. Strongly disagree ___e. Let's discuss

122. I believe women should always dress in a sexy way.

M: ___a. Strongly agree ___ b. Agree ___c. Disagree ___d. Strongly disagree ___e. Let's discuss
F: ___a. Strongly agree ___ b. Agree ___c. Disagree ___d. Strongly disagree ___e. Let's discuss

123. I believe women should always dress in a conservative way.

M: ___a. Strongly agree ___ b. Agree ___c. Disagree ___d. Strongly disagree ___e. Let's discuss
F: ___a. Strongly agree ___ b. Agree ___c. Disagree ___d. Strongly disagree ___e. Let's discuss

124. A woman should dress to please her man.

M: ___a. Strongly agree ___ b. Agree ___c. Disagree ___d. Strongly disagree ___e. Let's discuss
F: ___a. Strongly agree ___ b. Agree ___c. Disagree ___d. Strongly disagree ___e. Let's discuss

125. I believe there are *some* situations in which it is acceptable for a man or a woman to dress in a sexy way.

M: ___a. Strongly agree ___ b. Agree ___c. Disagree ___d. Strongly disagree ___e. Let's discuss
F: ___a. Strongly agree ___ b. Agree ___c. Disagree ___d. Strongly disagree ___e. Let's discuss

126. A man should dress to please his woman.

M: ___a. Strongly agree ___ b. Agree ___c. Disagree ___d. Strongly disagree ___e. Let's discuss
F: ___a. Strongly agree ___ b. Agree ___c. Disagree ___d. Strongly disagree ___e. Let's discuss

127. People should dress to please themselves.

M: ___a. Strongly agree ___ b. Agree ___c. Disagree ___d. Strongly disagree ___e. Let's discuss
F: ___a. Strongly agree ___ b. Agree ___c. Disagree ___d. Strongly disagree ___e. Let's discuss

128. I am not shy about my nudity.

M: ___a. Strongly agree ___ b. Agree ___c. Disagree ___d. Strongly disagree ___e. Let's discuss
F: ___a. Strongly agree ___ b. Agree ___c. Disagree ___d. Strongly disagree ___e. Let's discuss

Clothing

129. I often walk around nude at home.

M: ___a. Strongly agree   ___ b. Agree   ___c. Disagree   ___d. Strongly disagree   ___e. Let's discuss
F: ___a. Strongly agree   ___ b. Agree   ___c. Disagree   ___d. Strongly disagree   ___e. Let's discuss

130. I believe nudity is natural and beautiful.

M: ___a. Strongly agree   ___ b. Agree   ___c. Disagree   ___d. Strongly disagree   ___e. Let's discuss
F: ___a. Strongly agree   ___ b. Agree   ___c. Disagree   ___d. Strongly disagree   ___e. Let's discuss

131. It would bother me to have my partner walk around nude at home.

M: ___a. Strongly agree   ___ b. Agree   ___c. Disagree   ___d. Strongly disagree   ___e. Let's discuss
F: ___a. Strongly agree   ___ b. Agree   ___c. Disagree   ___d. Strongly disagree   ___e. Let's discuss

132. I would enjoy visiting a beach where clothing was optional.

M: ___a. Strongly agree   ___ b. Agree   ___c. Disagree   ___d. Strongly disagree   ___e. Let's discuss
F: ___a. Strongly agree   ___ b. Agree   ___c. Disagree   ___d. Strongly disagree   ___e. Let's discuss

133. I believe there should be laws to prevent women from walking around topless in public.

M: ___a. Strongly agree   ___ b. Agree   ___c. Disagree   ___d. Strongly disagree   ___e. Let's discuss
F: ___a. Strongly agree   ___ b. Agree   ___c. Disagree   ___d. Strongly disagree   ___e. Let's discuss

134. Mothers who nurse their infants in public are exhibitionists.

M: ___a. Strongly agree   ___ b. Agree   ___c. Disagree   ___d. Strongly disagree   ___e. Let's discuss
F: ___a. Strongly agree   ___ b. Agree   ___c. Disagree   ___d. Strongly disagree   ___e. Let's discuss

135. I am uncomfortable when I see nude art displayed in someone's home.

M: ___a. Strongly agree   ___ b. Agree   ___c. Disagree   ___d. Strongly disagree   ___e. Let's discuss
F: ___a. Strongly agree   ___ b. Agree   ___c. Disagree   ___d. Strongly disagree   ___e. Let's discuss

Shelter

Does your partner dream of living in a log cabin in the woods...or in a city loft apartment? Perhaps your partner loves contemporary homes and furnishings — or prefers roving flea markets for offbeat household accessories. Find out in this section.

DIRECTIONS: **IF you are a male,** place your check mark next to the response that most closely matches how much you agree or disagree with each statement. Select "Let's discuss" *only* if you believe the other answers are not appropriate. Place your check mark in the row opposite the "M," which stands for "male." **IF you are a female**, follow the same directions, except place your check mark on the row marked "F" for "female."

136. I prefer living in an apartment rather than a house.

M: ___a. Strongly agree ___ b. Agree ___c. Disagree ___d. Strongly disagree ___e. Let's discuss
F: ___a. Strongly agree ___ b. Agree ___c. Disagree ___d. Strongly disagree ___e. Let's discuss

137. It is important to own one's own home.

M: ___a. Strongly agree ___ b. Agree ___c. Disagree ___d. Strongly disagree ___e. Let's discuss
F: ___a. Strongly agree ___ b. Agree ___c. Disagree ___d. Strongly disagree ___e. Let's discuss

138. I enjoy doing basic plumbing work.

M: ___a. Strongly agree ___ b. Agree ___c. Disagree ___d. Strongly disagree ___e. Let's discuss
F: ___a. Strongly agree ___ b. Agree ___c. Disagree ___d. Strongly disagree ___e. Let's discuss

139. I enjoy doing basic electrical work.

M: ___a. Strongly agree ___ b. Agree ___c. Disagree ___d. Strongly disagree ___e. Let's discuss
F: ___a. Strongly agree ___ b. Agree ___c. Disagree ___d. Strongly disagree ___e. Let's discuss

140. I would like to live in a contemporary-style home.

M: ___a. Strongly agree ___ b. Agree ___c. Disagree ___d. Strongly disagree ___e. Let's discuss
F: ___a. Strongly agree ___ b. Agree ___c. Disagree ___d. Strongly disagree ___e. Let's discuss

141. I would like to live in a rustic-style home.

M: ___a. Strongly agree ___ b. Agree ___c. Disagree ___d. Strongly disagree ___e. Let's discuss
F: ___a. Strongly agree ___ b. Agree ___c. Disagree ___d. Strongly disagree ___e. Let's discuss

142. I like decorating my home with flea market and garage sale items.

M: ___a. Strongly agree ___ b. Agree ___c. Disagree ___d. Strongly disagree ___e. Let's discuss
F: ___a. Strongly agree ___ b. Agree ___c. Disagree ___d. Strongly disagree ___e. Let's discuss

143. It's important to have nice furniture, rugs, and wallpaper.

M: ___a. Strongly agree ___ b. Agree ___c. Disagree ___d. Strongly disagree ___e. Let's discuss
F: ___a. Strongly agree ___ b. Agree ___c. Disagree ___d. Strongly disagree ___e. Let's discuss

144. I prefer living in the country.

M: ___a. Strongly agree ___ b. Agree ___c. Disagree ___d. Strongly disagree ___e. Let's discuss
F: ___a. Strongly agree ___ b. Agree ___c. Disagree ___d. Strongly disagree ___e. Let's discuss

145. I prefer living in the city.

M: ___a. Strongly agree ___ b. Agree ___c. Disagree ___d. Strongly disagree ___e. Let's discuss
F: ___a. Strongly agree ___ b. Agree ___c. Disagree ___d. Strongly disagree ___e. Let's discuss

146. I prefer living in a suburban area.

M: ___a. Strongly agree ___ b. Agree ___c. Disagree ___d. Strongly disagree ___e. Let's discuss
F: ___a. Strongly agree ___ b. Agree ___c. Disagree ___d. Strongly disagree ___e. Let's discuss

147. I prefer antiques and old furniture with character.

M: ___a. Strongly agree ___ b. Agree ___c. Disagree ___d. Strongly disagree ___e. Let's discuss
F: ___a. Strongly agree ___ b. Agree ___c. Disagree ___d. Strongly disagree ___e. Let's discuss

148. I prefer purchasing new furniture and decorative accessories.

M: ___a. Strongly agree ___ b. Agree ___c. Disagree ___d. Strongly disagree ___e. Let's discuss
F: ___a. Strongly agree ___ b. Agree ___c. Disagree ___d. Strongly disagree ___e. Let's discuss

149. I like to spend a lot of time at home, fixing it up and making it look nice.

M: ___a. Strongly agree ___ b. Agree ___c. Disagree ___d. Strongly disagree ___e. Let's discuss
F: ___a. Strongly agree ___ b. Agree ___c. Disagree ___d. Strongly disagree ___e. Let's discuss

150. I prefer *not* to spend a lot of time at home.

M: ___a. Strongly agree ___ b. Agree ___c. Disagree ___d. Strongly disagree ___e. Let's discuss
F: ___a. Strongly agree ___ b. Agree ___c. Disagree ___d. Strongly disagree ___e. Let's discuss

151. I would prefer to go to a ball game, a festival, or practically any other event rather than stay home to redecorate or renovate my home.

M: ___a. Strongly agree ___ b. Agree ___c. Disagree ___d. Strongly disagree ___e. Let's discuss
F: ___a. Strongly agree ___ b. Agree ___c. Disagree ___d. Strongly disagree ___e. Let's discuss

E. Health

Smoking

If one of you smokes, and the other doesn't, you may have some arguments ahead of you. Even if you don't mind the odor or the health consequences, you may resent having the household budget eaten away by this expensive habit.

If you do smoke, consider quitting and joining the ever-growing legion of obnoxious ex-smokers. Instead of antagonizing non-smokers, you can begin a new hobby of antagonizing smokers. It'll be fun.

152. I smoke.

M: ___a. Yes ___ b. No ___c. Let's discuss
F: ___a. Yes ___ b. No ___c. Let's discuss

153. I would prefer that my partner not smoke.

M: ___a. Strongly agree ___ b. Agree ___c. Disagree ___d. Strongly disagree ___e. Let's discuss
F: ___a. Strongly agree ___ b. Agree ___c. Disagree ___d. Strongly disagree ___e. Let's discuss

154. I would stop dating a person if that person had no intention of quitting smoking some time in the near future.

M: ___a. Strongly agree ___ b. Agree ___c. Disagree ___d. Strongly disagree ___e. Let's discuss
F: ___a. Strongly agree ___ b. Agree ___c. Disagree ___d. Strongly disagree ___e. Let's discuss

41

155. A smoker's hair, clothes, car, and home often smell awful.

M: ___a. Strongly agree ___ b. Agree ___c. Disagree ___d. Strongly disagree ___e. Let's discuss
F: ___a. Strongly agree ___ b. Agree ___c. Disagree ___d. Strongly disagree ___e. Let's discuss

156. Smokers who can't quit have no will power.

M: ___a. Strongly agree ___ b. Agree ___c. Disagree ___d. Strongly disagree ___e. Let's discuss
F: ___a. Strongly agree ___ b. Agree ___c. Disagree ___d. Strongly disagree ___e. Let's discuss

157. Quitting smoking is extremely difficult.

M: ___a. Strongly agree ___ b. Agree ___c. Disagree ___d. Strongly disagree ___e. Let's discuss
F: ___a. Strongly agree ___ b. Agree ___c. Disagree ___d. Strongly disagree ___e. Let's discuss

158. I get angry when I am in a situation in which I must inhale others' cigarette smoke.

M: ___a. Strongly agree ___ b. Agree ___c. Disagree ___d. Strongly disagree ___e. Let's discuss
F: ___a. Strongly agree ___ b. Agree ___c. Disagree ___d. Strongly disagree ___e. Let's discuss

NOTE: *Answer the following five questions only if you are a smoker.*

159. I have no intention of quitting smoking.

M: ___a. Strongly agree ___ b. Agree ___c. Disagree ___d. Strongly disagree ___e. Let's discuss
F: ___a. Strongly agree ___ b. Agree ___c. Disagree ___d. Strongly disagree ___e. Let's discuss

160. As a smoker, I get angry at non-smokers who think they are the only ones with rights.

M: ___a. Strongly agree ___ b. Agree ___c. Disagree ___d. Strongly disagree ___e. Let's discuss
F: ___a. Strongly agree ___ b. Agree ___c. Disagree ___d. Strongly disagree ___e. Let's discuss

161. If I went to a friend's house for dinner and was asked not to smoke in the house, I would leave and not come back.

M: ___a. Strongly agree ___ b. Agree ___c. Disagree ___d. Strongly disagree ___e. Let's discuss
F: ___a. Strongly agree ___ b. Agree ___c. Disagree ___d. Strongly disagree ___e. Let's discuss

162. I try to be a considerate smoker and will not smoke around people who object to it.

M: ___a. Strongly agree ___ b. Agree ___c. Disagree ___d. Strongly disagree ___e. Let's discuss
F: ___a. Strongly agree ___ b. Agree ___c. Disagree ___d. Strongly disagree ___e. Let's discuss

163. I would like to quit smoking some time soon.

M: ___a. Strongly agree ___ b. Agree ___c. Disagree ___d. Strongly disagree ___e. Let's discuss
F: ___a. Strongly agree ___ b. Agree ___c. Disagree ___d. Strongly disagree ___e. Let's discuss

Drinking

The only thing I have to say about this subject is: *Please don't drink and drive.* Thank you.

Oh yes, and don't drink if you're taking particular types of prescription drugs...or at family gatherings...or if you have to work the next morning...or at company events if you need your job...or if you're pregnant...or if you're with anyone you're trying to impress.

I'm not saying you should never drink. An occasional glass of wine with dinner, or a cold beer on a hot day, are *wonderful* things.

164. I drink alcoholic beverages.

M: ___a. Strongly agree ___ b. Agree ___c. Disagree ___d. Strongly disagree ___e. Let's discuss
F: ___a. Strongly agree ___ b. Agree ___c. Disagree ___d. Strongly disagree ___e. Let's discuss

165. I have sought help for a drinking problem in the past.

M: ___a. Strongly agree ___ b. Agree ___c. Disagree ___d. Strongly disagree ___e. Let's discuss
F: ___a. Strongly agree ___ b. Agree ___c. Disagree ___d. Strongly disagree ___e. Let's discuss

166. I am an alcoholic.

M: ___a. Strongly agree ___ b. Agree ___c. Disagree ___d. Strongly disagree ___e. Let's discuss
F: ___a. Strongly agree ___ b. Agree ___c. Disagree ___d. Strongly disagree ___e. Let's discuss

Drinking

NOTE: *Answer the following questions in this section only if you drink alcoholic beverages.*

167. I would like to stop drinking.

M: ___a. Strongly agree ___ b. Agree ___c. Disagree ___d. Strongly disagree ___e. Let's discuss
F: ___a. Strongly agree ___ b. Agree ___c. Disagree ___d. Strongly disagree ___e. Let's discuss

168. I drink, but only socially.

M: ___a. Strongly agree ___ b. Agree ___c. Disagree ___d. Strongly disagree ___e. Let's discuss
F: ___a. Strongly agree ___ b. Agree ___c. Disagree ___d. Strongly disagree ___e. Let's discuss

169. I do not drink very much.

M: ___a. Strongly agree ___ b. Agree ___c. Disagree ___d. Strongly disagree ___e. Let's discuss
F: ___a. Strongly agree ___ b. Agree ___c. Disagree ___d. Strongly disagree ___e. Let's discuss

170. I drink, but only on weekends.

M: ___a. Strongly agree ___ b. Agree ___c. Disagree ___d. Strongly disagree ___e. Let's discuss
F: ___a. Strongly agree ___ b. Agree ___c. Disagree ___d. Strongly disagree ___e. Let's discuss

171. I drink a little almost every day.

M: ___a. Strongly agree ___ b. Agree ___c. Disagree ___d. Strongly disagree ___e. Let's discuss
F: ___a. Strongly agree ___ b. Agree ___c. Disagree ___d. Strongly disagree ___e. Let's discuss

172. When I go out to a bar, restaurant, or social gathering, I usually have six or more alcoholic drinks.

M: ___a. Strongly agree ___ b. Agree ___c. Disagree ___d. Strongly disagree ___e. Let's discuss
F: ___a. Strongly agree ___ b. Agree ___c. Disagree ___d. Strongly disagree ___e. Let's discuss

173. When I go out to a bar, restaurant, or social gathering, I rarely have more than two drinks.

M: ___a. Strongly agree ___ b. Agree ___c. Disagree ___d. Strongly disagree ___e. Let's discuss
F: ___a. Strongly agree ___ b. Agree ___c. Disagree ___d. Strongly disagree ___e. Let's discuss

174. If I drink, I usually drink at home.

M: ___a. Strongly agree ___ b. Agree ___c. Disagree ___d. Strongly disagree ___e. Let's discuss
F: ___a. Strongly agree ___ b. Agree ___c. Disagree ___d. Strongly disagree ___e. Let's discuss

175. I usually have no more than two drinks a day when I drink at home.

M: ___a. Strongly agree ___ b. Agree ___c. Disagree ___d. Strongly disagree ___e. Let's discuss
F: ___a. Strongly agree ___ b. Agree ___c. Disagree ___d. Strongly disagree ___e. Let's discuss

176. It is no one's business how much I drink.

M: ___a. Strongly agree ___ b. Agree ___c. Disagree ___d. Strongly disagree ___e. Let's discuss
F: ___a. Strongly agree ___ b. Agree ___c. Disagree ___d. Strongly disagree ___e. Let's discuss

177. In the past, I have been arrested for driving while intoxicated or driving under the influence of alcohol.

M: ___a. Yes ___ b. No ___c. Let's discuss
F: ___a. Yes ___ b. No ___c. Let's discuss

178. I would end our relationship if my partner was an alcoholic who refused to obtain help.

M: ___a. Strongly agree ___ b. Agree ___c. Disagree ___d. Strongly disagree ___e. Let's discuss
F: ___a. Strongly agree ___ b. Agree ___c. Disagree ___d. Strongly disagree ___e. Let's discuss

Drug Use

Would it bother you if your partner used illegal drugs? Would you tolerate marijuana but end the relationship if your loved one used cocaine? Is it okay to use drugs as long as you do it only occasionally — say at parties? Or would you walk out the door if you found your partner was a drug user? Find out in this section.

Drug Use

DIRECTIONS: **IF you are a male,** place your check mark next to the response that most closely matches how much you agree or disagree with each statement. Select "Let's discuss" *only* if you believe the other answers are not appropriate. Place your checkmark in the row opposite the "M," which stands for "male." **IF you are a female,** follow the same directions, except place your checkmark on the row marked "F" for "female."

179. If offered marijuana at a party, I would smoke it.

M: ___a. Strongly agree ___ b. Agree ___c. Disagree ___d. Strongly disagree ___e. Let's discuss
F: ___a. Strongly agree ___ b. Agree ___c. Disagree ___d. Strongly disagree ___e. Let's discuss

180. If given an opportunity, I would purchase illegal drugs.

M: ___a. Strongly agree ___ b. Agree ___c. Disagree ___d. Strongly disagree ___e. Let's discuss
F: ___a. Strongly agree ___ b. Agree ___c. Disagree ___d. Strongly disagree ___e. Let's discuss

181. If I found my partner used illegal drugs, I would end our relationship.

M: ___a. Strongly agree ___ b. Agree ___c. Disagree ___d. Strongly disagree ___e. Let's discuss
F: ___a. Strongly agree ___ b. Agree ___c. Disagree ___d. Strongly disagree ___e. Let's discuss

182. If given an opportunity, I would try LSD, heroine, cocaine, or other drugs to see what all the fuss was about.

M: ___a. Strongly agree ___ b. Agree ___c. Disagree ___d. Strongly disagree ___e. Let's discuss
F: ___a. Strongly agree ___ b. Agree ___c. Disagree ___d. Strongly disagree ___e. Let's discuss

183. Illegal drugs are not worth taking.

M: ___a. Strongly agree ___ b. Agree ___c. Disagree ___d. Strongly disagree ___e. Let's discuss
F: ___a. Strongly agree ___ b. Agree ___c. Disagree ___d. Strongly disagree ___e. Let's discuss

184. Drugs should be legalized.

M: ___a. Strongly agree ___ b. Agree ___c. Disagree ___d. Strongly disagree ___e. Let's discuss
F: ___a. Strongly agree ___ b. Agree ___c. Disagree ___d. Strongly disagree ___e. Let's discuss

185. I do not take (illegal) drugs.

M: ___a. Strongly agree ___ b. Agree ___c. Disagree ___d. Strongly disagree ___e. Let's discuss
F: ___a. Strongly agree ___ b. Agree ___c. Disagree ___d. Strongly disagree ___e. Let's discuss

Drug Use

186. Some of my friends take drugs.

M: ___a. Strongly agree ___ b. Agree ___c. Disagree ___d. Strongly disagree ___e. Let's discuss
F: ___a. Strongly agree ___ b. Agree ___c. Disagree ___d. Strongly disagree ___e. Let's discuss

Emotional Health

You may find this section more difficult to complete than other sections. If you feel uncomfortable answering some questions, select the "Let's discuss" option.

DIRECTIONS: **IF you are a male,** place your check mark next to the response that most closely matches how much you agree or disagree with each statement. Select "Let's discuss" *only* if you believe the other answers are not appropriate. Place your check mark in the row opposite the "M," which stands for "male." **IF you are a female,** follow the same directions, except place your check mark on the row marked "F" for "female."

187. I don't often get angry.

M: ___a. Strongly agree ___ b. Agree ___c. Disagree ___d. Strongly disagree ___e. Let's discuss
F: ___a. Strongly agree ___ b. Agree ___c. Disagree ___d. Strongly disagree ___e. Let's discuss

188. If I get angry about something, I try not to let it bother me too much.

M: ___a. Strongly agree ___ b. Agree ___c. Disagree ___d. Strongly disagree ___e. Let's discuss
F: ___a. Strongly agree ___ b. Agree ___c. Disagree ___d. Strongly disagree ___e. Let's discuss

189. When I get really angry, most people can't tell how angry I am because I try not to let it show.

M: ___a. Strongly agree ___ b. Agree ___c. Disagree ___d. Strongly disagree ___e. Let's discuss
F: ___a. Strongly agree ___ b. Agree ___c. Disagree ___d. Strongly disagree ___e. Let's discuss

47

190. I often get angry at the people for whom I work.

M: ___a. Strongly agree ___ b. Agree ___c. Disagree ___d. Strongly disagree ___e. Let's discuss
F: ___a. Strongly agree ___ b. Agree ___c. Disagree ___d. Strongly disagree ___e. Let's discuss

191. I often get angry at my co-workers.

M: ___a. Strongly agree ___ b. Agree ___c. Disagree ___d. Strongly disagree ___e. Let's discuss
F: ___a. Strongly agree ___ b. Agree ___c. Disagree ___d. Strongly disagree ___e. Let's discuss

192. I have been arrested before.

M: ___a. Strongly agree ___ b. Agree ___c. Disagree ___d. Strongly disagree ___e. Let's discuss
F: ___a. Strongly agree ___ b. Agree ___c. Disagree ___d. Strongly disagree ___e. Let's discuss

193. I have spent time in jail.

M: ___a. Strongly agree ___ b. Agree ___c. Disagree ___d. Strongly disagree ___e. Let's discuss
F: ___a. Strongly agree ___ b. Agree ___c. Disagree ___d. Strongly disagree ___e. Let's discuss

194. I have been told that I have a quick temper.

M: ___a. Strongly agree ___ b. Agree ___c. Disagree ___d. Strongly disagree ___e. Let's discuss
F: ___a. Strongly agree ___ b. Agree ___c. Disagree ___d. Strongly disagree ___e. Let's discuss

195. I have hit someone before.

M: ___a. Strongly agree ___ b. Agree ___c. Disagree ___d. Strongly disagree ___e. Let's discuss
F: ___a. Strongly agree ___ b. Agree ___c. Disagree ___d. Strongly disagree ___e. Let's discuss

196. I have destroyed objects during outbursts of anger.

M: ___a. Strongly agree ___ b. Agree ___c. Disagree ___d. Strongly disagree ___e. Let's discuss
F: ___a. Strongly agree ___ b. Agree ___c. Disagree ___d. Strongly disagree ___e. Let's discuss

197. If my spouse and I were in a bar, and an intoxicate person continued to harass my spouse after being asked to stop, I would punch the person if I had to.

M: ___a. Strongly agree ___ b. Agree ___c. Disagree ___d. Strongly disagree ___e. Let's discuss
F: ___a. Strongly agree ___ b. Agree ___c. Disagree ___d. Strongly disagree ___e. Let's discuss

198. I think I handle stress very well.

M: ___ a. Strongly agree ___ b. Agree ___ c. Disagree ___ d. Strongly disagree ___ e. Let's discuss
F: ___ a. Strongly agree ___ b. Agree ___ c. Disagree ___ d. Strongly disagree ___ e. Let's discuss

199. If my partner ever physically abused me, even *once*, I would immediately end the relationship.

M: ___ a. Strongly agree ___ b. Agree ___ c. Disagree ___ d. Strongly disagree ___ e. Let's discuss
F: ___ a. Strongly agree ___ b. Agree ___ c. Disagree ___ d. Strongly disagree ___ e. Let's discuss

200. I think psychological therapy can be very beneficial for some people.

M: ___ a. Strongly agree ___ b. Agree ___ c. Disagree ___ d. Strongly disagree ___ e. Let's discuss
F: ___ a. Strongly agree ___ b. Agree ___ c. Disagree ___ d. Strongly disagree ___ e. Let's discuss

201. I am in therapy now.

M: ___ a. Yes ___ b. No ___ c. Let's discuss
F: ___ a. Yes ___ b. No ___ c. Let's discuss

202. If my relationship with my partner was in trouble, I would not hesitate to seek professional counseling.

M: ___ a. Strongly agree ___ b. Agree ___ c. Disagree ___ d. Strongly disagree ___ e. Let's discuss
F: ___ a. Strongly agree ___ b. Agree ___ c. Disagree ___ d. Strongly disagree ___ e. Let's discuss

203. If I my partner emotionally abused me, and if my partner would not participate in counseling, I would most likely end the relationship.

M: ___ a. Strongly agree ___ b. Agree ___ c. Disagree ___ d. Strongly disagree ___ e. Let's discuss
F: ___ a. Strongly agree ___ b. Agree ___ c. Disagree ___ d. Strongly disagree ___ e. Let's discuss

204. I take, or have taken, anti-depressant medication or other mood-altering drug(s).

M: ___a. Yes ___ b. No ___c. Let's discuss
F: ___a. Yes ___ b. No ___c. Let's discuss

205. I like to talk with my partner about my feelings.

M: ___a. Yes ___ b. No ___c. Let's discuss
F: ___a. Yes ___ b. No ___c. Let's discuss

F. Sex

Ah! Sex! Did you turn to this section first, before all others? Not surprising. This is one subject that a lot of people have trouble discussing. It's often difficult to communicate your needs without sounding as if you are complaining, right? Wouldn't it be *wonderful* if your partner could just read your mind? But unless your partner is an extraterrestrial, that's not likely to happen.

You may find that you are compatible in all areas except this one. Or perhaps you'll find you're compatible *only* in this area. It happens.

DIRECTIONS: **IF you are a male,** place your check mark next to the response that most closely matches how much you agree or disagree with each statement. Select "Let's discuss" *only* if you believe the other answers are not appropriate. Place your checkmark in the row opposite the "M," which stands for "male." **IF you are a female**, follow the same directions, except place your checkmark on the row marked "F" for "female."

206. A lovemaking session usually lasts about a half hour or less.

M: ___ a. Strongly agree ___ b. Agree ___ c. Disagree ___ d. Strongly disagree ___ e. Let's discuss
F: ___ a. Strongly agree ___ b. Agree ___ c. Disagree ___ d. Strongly disagree ___ e. Let's discuss

207. A lovemaking session can last for hours.

M: ___ a. Strongly agree ___ b. Agree ___ c. Disagree ___ d. Strongly disagree ___ e. Let's discuss
F: ___ a. Strongly agree ___ b. Agree ___ c. Disagree ___ d. Strongly disagree ___ e. Let's discuss

208. A lovemaking session can last for days.

M: ___ a. Strongly agree ___ b. Agree ___ c. Disagree ___ d. Strongly disagree ___ e. Let's discuss
F: ___ a. Strongly agree ___ b. Agree ___ c. Disagree ___ d. Strongly disagree ___ e. Let's discuss

Sex

209. I am most comfortable making love in the morning.

M: ___a. Strongly agree ___ b. Agree ___c. Disagree ___d. Strongly disagree ___e. Let's discuss
F: ___a. Strongly agree ___ b. Agree ___c. Disagree ___d. Strongly disagree ___e. Let's discuss

210. I am most comfortable making love in the late evening.

M: ___a. Strongly agree ___ b. Agree ___c. Disagree ___d. Strongly disagree ___e. Let's discuss
F: ___a. Strongly agree ___ b. Agree ___c. Disagree ___d. Strongly disagree ___e. Let's discuss

211. I am most comfortable making love in the afternoon.

M: ___a. Strongly agree ___ b. Agree ___c. Disagree ___d. Strongly disagree ___e. Let's discuss
F: ___a. Strongly agree ___ b. Agree ___c. Disagree ___d. Strongly disagree ___e. Let's discuss

212. I am most comfortable making love during the weekend rather than during the week.

M: ___a. Strongly agree ___ b. Agree ___c. Disagree ___d. Strongly disagree ___e. Let's discuss
F: ___a. Strongly agree ___ b. Agree ___c. Disagree ___d. Strongly disagree ___e. Let's discuss

213. I believe any time is a good time for making love.

M: ___a. Strongly agree ___ b. Agree ___c. Disagree ___d. Strongly disagree ___e. Let's discuss
F: ___a. Strongly agree ___ b. Agree ___c. Disagree ___d. Strongly disagree ___e. Let's discuss

214. Any sex is good sex.

M: ___a. Strongly agree ___ b. Agree ___c. Disagree ___d. Strongly disagree ___e. Let's discuss
F: ___a. Strongly agree ___ b. Agree ___c. Disagree ___d. Strongly disagree ___e. Let's discuss

215. When women say "No," sometimes they mean "Yes."

M: ___a. Strongly agree ___ b. Agree ___c. Disagree ___d. Strongly disagree ___e. Let's discuss
F: ___a. Strongly agree ___ b. Agree ___c. Disagree ___d. Strongly disagree ___e. Let's discuss

216. Birth control is the responsibility of the woman *and* the man.

M: ___a. Strongly agree ___ b. Agree ___c. Disagree ___d. Strongly disagree ___e. Let's discuss
F: ___a. Strongly agree ___ b. Agree ___c. Disagree ___d. Strongly disagree ___e. Let's discuss

217. These days it is absolutely necessary to use condoms, regardless of how nice the person seems.

M: ___ a. Strongly agree ___ b. Agree ___ c. Disagree ___ d. Strongly disagree ___ e. Let's discuss
F: ___ a. Strongly agree ___ b. Agree ___ c. Disagree ___ d. Strongly disagree ___ e. Let's discuss

218. For men: If a woman is not using some form of birth control, and we are ready to make love, that's *her* problem.

M: ___ a. Strongly agree ___ b. Agree ___ c. Disagree ___ d. Strongly disagree ___ e. Let's discuss
F: ___ a. Strongly agree ___ b. Agree ___ c. Disagree ___ d. Strongly disagree ___ e. Let's discuss

219. If a person does not enjoy sex, I don't want a relationship with that person.

M: ___ a. Strongly agree ___ b. Agree ___ c. Disagree ___ d. Strongly disagree ___ e. Let's discuss
F: ___ a. Strongly agree ___ b. Agree ___ c. Disagree ___ d. Strongly disagree ___ e. Let's discuss

220. It's a good idea to talk about sex with my partner.

M: ___ a. Strongly agree ___ b. Agree ___ c. Disagree ___ d. Strongly disagree ___ e. Let's discuss
F: ___ a. Strongly agree ___ b. Agree ___ c. Disagree ___ d. Strongly disagree ___ e. Let's discuss

221. I like to laugh when making love.

M: ___ a. Strongly agree ___ b. Agree ___ c. Disagree ___ d. Strongly disagree ___ e. Let's discuss
F: ___ a. Strongly agree ___ b. Agree ___ c. Disagree ___ d. Strongly disagree ___ e. Let's discuss

222. Talking about sex ruins the mood.

M: ___ a. Strongly agree ___ b. Agree ___ c. Disagree ___ d. Strongly disagree ___ e. Let's discuss
F: ___ a. Strongly agree ___ b. Agree ___ c. Disagree ___ d. Strongly disagree ___ e. Let's discuss

223. I wish my partner didn't want to talk to me after we make love; it's normal for a person to want to go to sleep.

M: ___ a. Strongly agree ___ b. Agree ___ c. Disagree ___ d. Strongly disagree ___ e. Let's discuss
F: ___ a. Strongly agree ___ b. Agree ___ c. Disagree ___ d. Strongly disagree ___ e. Let's discuss

224. Oral sex is an acceptable sexual activity.

M: ___a. Strongly agree ___ b. Agree ___c. Disagree ___d. Strongly disagree ___e. Let's discuss
F: ___a. Strongly agree ___ b. Agree ___c. Disagree ___d. Strongly disagree ___e. Let's discuss

225. Anal sex is an acceptable sexual activity.

M: ___a. Strongly agree ___ b. Agree ___c. Disagree ___d. Strongly disagree ___e. Let's discuss
F: ___a. Strongly agree ___ b. Agree ___c. Disagree ___d. Strongly disagree ___e. Let's discuss

226. Making love more than three times a week is too often.

M: ___a. Strongly agree ___ b. Agree ___c. Disagree ___d. Strongly disagree ___e. Let's discuss
F: ___a. Strongly agree ___ b. Agree ___c. Disagree ___d. Strongly disagree ___e. Let's discuss

227. I am satisfied with sex once a month.

M: ___a. Strongly agree ___ b. Agree ___c. Disagree ___d. Strongly disagree ___e. Let's discuss
F: ___a. Strongly agree ___ b. Agree ___c. Disagree ___d. Strongly disagree ___e. Let's discuss

228. I am satisfied with daily sex.

M: ___a. Strongly agree ___ b. Agree ___c. Disagree ___d. Strongly disagree ___e. Let's discuss
F: ___a. Strongly agree ___ b. Agree ___c. Disagree ___d. Strongly disagree ___e. Let's discuss

229. I am satisfied if I have sex once a week.

M: ___a. Strongly agree ___ b. Agree ___c. Disagree ___d. Strongly disagree ___e. Let's discuss
F: ___a. Strongly agree ___ b. Agree ___c. Disagree ___d. Strongly disagree ___e. Let's discuss

230. I enjoy giving oral sex.

M: ___a. Strongly agree ___ b. Agree ___c. Disagree ___d. Strongly disagree ___e. Let's discuss
F: ___a. Strongly agree ___ b. Agree ___c. Disagree ___d. Strongly disagree ___e. Let's discuss

231. I enjoy receiving oral sex.

M: ___a. Strongly agree ___ b. Agree ___c. Disagree ___d. Strongly disagree ___e. Let's discuss
F: ___a. Strongly agree ___ b. Agree ___c. Disagree ___d. Strongly disagree ___e. Let's discuss

232. I don't care if I ever have sex again.

M: ___a. Strongly agree ___ b. Agree ___c. Disagree ___d. Strongly disagree ___e. Let's discuss
F: ___a. Strongly agree ___ b. Agree ___c. Disagree ___d. Strongly disagree ___e. Let's discuss

233. **I would not have sex with someone who did not take a daily bath or shower.**

M: ___a. Strongly agree   ___ b. Agree   ___c. Disagree   ___d. Strongly disagree   ___e. Let's discuss
F: ___a. Strongly agree   ___ b. Agree   ___c. Disagree   ___d. Strongly disagree   ___e. Let's discuss

234. **Sex is not that important to me.**

M: ___a. Strongly agree   ___ b. Agree   ___c. Disagree   ___d. Strongly disagree   ___e. Let's discuss
F: ___a. Strongly agree   ___ b. Agree   ___c. Disagree   ___d. Strongly disagree   ___e. Let's discuss

235. **A couple must be honest in sharing their thoughts about sex.**

M: ___a. Strongly agree   ___ b. Agree   ___c. Disagree   ___d. Strongly disagree   ___e. Let's discuss
F: ___a. Strongly agree   ___ b. Agree   ___c. Disagree   ___d. Strongly disagree   ___e. Let's discuss

236. **If women have trouble achieving orgasm, it's because they have hang-ups about sex.**

M: ___a. Strongly agree   ___ b. Agree   ___c. Disagree   ___d. Strongly disagree   ___e. Let's discuss
F: ___a. Strongly agree   ___ b. Agree   ___c. Disagree   ___d. Strongly disagree   ___e. Let's discuss

237. **I am an excellent lover, and I need no suggestions for improvement.**

M: ___a. Strongly agree   ___ b. Agree   ___c. Disagree   ___d. Strongly disagree   ___e. Let's discuss
F: ___a. Strongly agree   ___ b. Agree   ___c. Disagree   ___d. Strongly disagree   ___e. Let's discuss

238. **It is important to me to know exactly what pleases my lover during lovemaking.**

M: ___a. Strongly agree   ___ b. Agree   ___c. Disagree   ___d. Strongly disagree   ___e. Let's discuss
F: ___a. Strongly agree   ___ b. Agree   ___c. Disagree   ___d. Strongly disagree   ___e. Let's discuss

239. **If my partner and I were experiencing sexual dysfunction of any kind, I would not hesitate to attend counseling sessions with my partner.**

M: ___a. Strongly agree   ___ b. Agree   ___c. Disagree   ___d. Strongly disagree   ___e. Let's discuss
F: ___a. Strongly agree   ___ b. Agree   ___c. Disagree   ___d. Strongly disagree   ___e. Let's discuss

240. Masturbation is only for people who can't get sex any other way.

M: ___a. Strongly agree ___ b. Agree ___c. Disagree ___d. Strongly disagree ___e. Let's discuss
F: ___a. Strongly agree ___ b. Agree ___c. Disagree ___d. Strongly disagree ___e. Let's discuss

241. Many males do not fully understand basic female anatomy.

M: ___a. Strongly agree ___ b. Agree ___c. Disagree ___d. Strongly disagree ___e. Let's discuss
F: ___a. Strongly agree ___ b. Agree ___c. Disagree ___d. Strongly disagree ___e. Let's discuss

242. Masturbation is a normal and healthy sexual activity for anyone.

M: ___a. Strongly agree ___ b. Agree ___c. Disagree ___d. Strongly disagree ___e. Let's discuss
F: ___a. Strongly agree ___ b. Agree ___c. Disagree ___d. Strongly disagree ___e. Let's discuss

243. If I found out my partner masturbated, I would feel hurt and insulted.

M: ___a. Strongly agree ___ b. Agree ___c. Disagree ___d. Strongly disagree ___e. Let's discuss
F: ___a. Strongly agree ___ b. Agree ___c. Disagree ___d. Strongly disagree ___e. Let's discuss

244. The "missionary" style of sex is the best position for both men and women.

M: ___a. Strongly agree ___ b. Agree ___c. Disagree ___d. Strongly disagree ___e. Let's discuss
F: ___a. Strongly agree ___ b. Agree ___c. Disagree ___d. Strongly disagree ___e. Let's discuss

245. I would be insulted if my partner suggested I change my lovemaking techniques.

M: ___a. Strongly agree ___ b. Agree ___c. Disagree ___d. Strongly disagree ___e. Let's discuss
F: ___a. Strongly agree ___ b. Agree ___c. Disagree ___d. Strongly disagree ___e. Let's discuss

246. I would expect *my partner* to tell me, before we made love, if *he* or *she* had ever been infected with an incurable sexually transmitted disease such as herpes.

M: ___a. Strongly agree ___ b. Agree ___c. Disagree ___d. Strongly disagree ___e. Let's discuss
F: ___a. Strongly agree ___ b. Agree ___c. Disagree ___d. Strongly disagree ___e. Let's discuss

247. *I* would tell my partner, before we made love, if *I* had ever been infected with an incurable sexually transmitted disease such as herpes.

M: ___a. Strongly agree ___ b. Agree ___c. Disagree ___d. Strongly disagree ___e. Let's discuss
F: ___a. Strongly agree ___ b. Agree ___c. Disagree ___d. Strongly disagree ___e. Let's discuss

248. If *I* had AIDS or had been exposed to AIDS, I would tell my partner immediately (and most definitely before making love).

M: ___a. Strongly agree ___ b. Agree ___c. Disagree ___d. Strongly disagree ___e. Let's discuss
F: ___a. Strongly agree ___ b. Agree ___c. Disagree ___d. Strongly disagree ___e. Let's discuss

249. If *my partner* had been exposed to AIDS, I would expect my partner to tell me immediately (and most definitely before making love).

M: ___a. Strongly agree ___ b. Agree ___c. Disagree ___d. Strongly disagree ___e. Let's discuss
F: ___a. Strongly agree ___ b. Agree ___c. Disagree ___d. Strongly disagree ___e. Let's discuss

250. If I found I had been exposed to *any* sexually transmitted disease (incurable or not), I would immediately tell my partner (definitely before making love) and would expect my partner to do the same.

M: ___a. Strongly agree ___ b. Agree ___c. Disagree ___d. Strongly disagree ___e. Let's discuss
F: ___a. Strongly agree ___ b. Agree ___c. Disagree ___d. Strongly disagree ___e. Let's discuss

251. I have a disease or condition that can be transmitted sexually.

M: ___a. Strongly agree ___ b. Agree ___c. Disagree ___d. Strongly disagree ___e. Let's discuss
F: ___a. Strongly agree ___ b. Agree ___c. Disagree ___d. Strongly disagree ___e. Let's discuss

252. I have a disease or condition that can be transmitted sexually that is now dormant and is not now contagious.

M: ___a. Strongly agree ___ b. Agree ___c. Disagree ___d. Strongly disagree ___e. Let's discuss
F: ___a. Strongly agree ___ b. Agree ___c. Disagree ___d. Strongly disagree ___e. Let's discuss

253. I will not begin a sexual relationship unless my partner and I have both been tested for the AIDS virus.

M: ___a. Strongly agree ___ b. Agree ___c. Disagree ___d. Strongly disagree ___e. Let's discuss
F: ___a. Strongly agree ___ b. Agree ___c. Disagree ___d. Strongly disagree ___e. Let's discuss

254. I have the AIDS virus.

M: ___a. Yes ___ b. No ___c. Let's discuss
F: ___a. Yes ___ b. No ___c. Let's discuss

255. I am HIV Positive.

M: ___a. Yes ___ b. No ___c. Let's discuss
F: ___a. Yes ___ b. No ___c. Let's discuss

256. I have been tested for the AIDS virus in the past.

M: ___a. Yes ___ b. No ___c. Let's discuss
F: ___a. Yes ___ b. No ___c. Let's discuss

257. Abortion should remain legal.

M: ___a. Strongly agree ___ b. Agree ___c. Disagree ___d. Strongly disagree ___e. Let's discuss
F: ___a. Strongly agree ___ b. Agree ___c. Disagree ___d. Strongly disagree ___e. Let's discuss

258. For men: If my partner became pregnant, I would not object to an abortion if she wished to obtain one.

M: ___a. Strongly agree ___ b. Agree ___c. Disagree ___d. Strongly disagree ___e. Let's discuss
F: ___a. Strongly agree ___ b. Agree ___c. Disagree ___d. Strongly disagree ___e. Let's discuss

259. For men: If my partner became pregnant, I would try to prevent an abortion and would want to become involved in the child's life.

M: ___a. Strongly agree ___ b. Agree ___c. Disagree ___d. Strongly disagree ___e. Let's discuss
F: ___a. Strongly agree ___ b. Agree ___c. Disagree ___d. Strongly disagree ___e. Let's discuss

260. **For men: If my partner became pregnant, the decision to have the baby or not would be her decision, and I would support whatever decision she made.**

M: ___a. Strongly agree ___ b. Agree ___c. Disagree ___d. Strongly disagree ___e. Let's discuss
F: ___a. Strongly agree ___ b. Agree ___c. Disagree ___d. Strongly disagree ___e. Let's discuss

261. **For women: If I became pregnant, I would probably have an abortion.**

M: ___a. Strongly agree ___ b. Agree ___c. Disagree ___d. Strongly disagree ___e. Let's discuss
F: ___a. Strongly agree ___ b. Agree ___c. Disagree ___d. Strongly disagree ___e. Let's discuss

262. **For women: If I became pregnant, I would never have an abortion; I would give birth to the child.**

M: ___a. Strongly agree ___ b. Agree ___c. Disagree ___d. Strongly disagree ___e. Let's discuss
F: ___a. Strongly agree ___ b. Agree ___c. Disagree ___d. Strongly disagree ___e. Let's discuss

263. **For women: If I became pregnant, I believe my partner would have no say in whether I continued the pregnancy.**

M: ___a. Strongly agree ___ b. Agree ___c. Disagree ___d. Strongly disagree ___e. Let's discuss
F: ___a. Strongly agree ___ b. Agree ___c. Disagree ___d. Strongly disagree ___e. Let's discuss

264. **The decision to have a child is the woman's choice alone.**

M: ___a. Strongly agree ___ b. Agree ___c. Disagree ___d. Strongly disagree ___e. Let's discuss
F: ___a. Strongly agree ___ b. Agree ___c. Disagree ___d. Strongly disagree ___e. Let's discuss

265. **I would not have sex with someone unless we used a condom.**

M: ___a. Strongly agree ___ b. Agree ___c. Disagree ___d. Strongly disagree ___e. Let's discuss
F: ___a. Strongly agree ___ b. Agree ___c. Disagree ___d. Strongly disagree ___e. Let's discuss

266. **It is extremely important for a man and women to discuss birth control methods before having sex.**

M: ___a. Strongly agree ___ b. Agree ___c. Disagree ___d. Strongly disagree ___e. Let's discuss
F: ___a. Strongly agree ___ b. Agree ___c. Disagree ___d. Strongly disagree ___e. Let's discuss

267. There is no such thing as 100% safe sex.

M: ___a. Strongly agree ___ b. Agree ___c. Disagree ___d. Strongly disagree ___e. Let's discuss
F: ___a. Strongly agree ___ b. Agree ___c. Disagree ___d. Strongly disagree ___e. Let's discuss

268. Some sexually transmitted diseases can be transmitted even when a condom is used.

M: ___a. Strongly agree ___ b. Agree ___c. Disagree ___d. Strongly disagree ___e. Let's discuss
F: ___a. Strongly agree ___ b. Agree ___c. Disagree ___d. Strongly disagree ___e. Let's discuss

269. If my partner wanted me to wear sexy lingerie/pajamas in bed, I would have no problem with that.

M: ___a. Strongly agree ___ b. Agree ___c. Disagree ___d. Strongly disagree ___e. Let's discuss
F: ___a. Strongly agree ___ b. Agree ___c. Disagree ___d. Strongly disagree ___e. Let's discuss

270. I enjoy wearing sexy lingerie/pajamas.

M: ___a. Strongly agree ___ b. Agree ___c. Disagree ___d. Strongly disagree ___e. Let's discuss
F: ___a. Strongly agree ___ b. Agree ___c. Disagree ___d. Strongly disagree ___e. Let's discuss

271. I enjoy having my partner wear sexy lingerie/pajamas.

M: ___a. Strongly agree ___ b. Agree ___c. Disagree ___d. Strongly disagree ___e. Let's discuss
F: ___a. Strongly agree ___ b. Agree ___c. Disagree ___d. Strongly disagree ___e. Let's discuss

272. If my partner wanted to dress up in clothes of the opposite sex, I would have no problem with that.

M: ___a. Strongly agree ___ b. Agree ___c. Disagree ___d. Strongly disagree ___e. Let's discuss
F: ___a. Strongly agree ___ b. Agree ___c. Disagree ___d. Strongly disagree ___e. Let's discuss

273. For women: if my partner wanted me to dress up in an outfit other than traditional sexy lingerie, I would have no problem with that.

M: ___a. Strongly agree ___ b. Agree ___c. Disagree ___d. Strongly disagree ___e. Let's discuss
F: ___a. Strongly agree ___ b. Agree ___c. Disagree ___d. Strongly disagree ___e. Let's discuss

274. Women need more foreplay than men.

M: ___a. Strongly agree ___ b. Agree ___c. Disagree ___d. Strongly disagree ___e. Let's discuss
F: ___a. Strongly agree ___ b. Agree ___c. Disagree ___d. Strongly disagree ___e. Let's discuss

275. Sex gadgets are okay for those who enjoy them.

M: ___a. Strongly agree ___ b. Agree ___c. Disagree ___d. Strongly disagree ___e. Let's discuss
F: ___a. Strongly agree ___ b. Agree ___c. Disagree ___d. Strongly disagree ___e. Let's discuss

276. Sex gadgets are disgusting.

M: ___a. Strongly agree ___ b. Agree ___c. Disagree ___d. Strongly disagree ___e. Let's discuss
F: ___a. Strongly agree ___ b. Agree ___c. Disagree ___d. Strongly disagree ___e. Let's discuss

277. For men: I would be angry if I found my partner used a vibrator.

M: ___a. Strongly agree ___ b. Agree ___c. Disagree ___d. Strongly disagree ___e. Let's discuss
F: ___a. Strongly agree ___ b. Agree ___c. Disagree ___d. Strongly disagree ___e. Let's discuss

278. Anything that can enhance the sexual experience is okay by me.

M: ___a. Strongly agree ___ b. Agree ___c. Disagree ___d. Strongly disagree ___e. Let's discuss
F: ___a. Strongly agree ___ b. Agree ___c. Disagree ___d. Strongly disagree ___e. Let's discuss

279. Playing sex games can be fun if both parties agree to them.

M: ___a. Strongly agree ___ b. Agree ___c. Disagree ___d. Strongly disagree ___e. Let's discuss
F: ___a. Strongly agree ___ b. Agree ___c. Disagree ___d. Strongly disagree ___e. Let's discuss

280. I enjoy sex games that simulate violence.

M: ___a. Strongly agree ___ b. Agree ___c. Disagree ___d. Strongly disagree ___e. Let's discuss
F: ___a. Strongly agree ___ b. Agree ___c. Disagree ___d. Strongly disagree ___e. Let's discuss

281. If my partner wanted to play sex games that were violent or simulated violence, I would refuse to participate.

M: ___a. Strongly agree ___ b. Agree ___c. Disagree ___d. Strongly disagree ___e. Let's discuss
F: ___a. Strongly agree ___ b. Agree ___c. Disagree ___d. Strongly disagree ___e. Let's discuss

282. People who have sexual fantasies are not normal.

M: ___a. Strongly agree ___ b. Agree ___c. Disagree ___d. Strongly disagree ___e. Let's discuss
F: ___a. Strongly agree ___ b. Agree ___c. Disagree ___d. Strongly disagree ___e. Let's discuss

283. Sexual fantasies are harmless.

M: ___a. Strongly agree ___ b. Agree ___c. Disagree ___d. Strongly disagree ___e. Let's discuss
F: ___a. Strongly agree ___ b. Agree ___c. Disagree ___d. Strongly disagree ___e. Let's discuss

284. Discussing sexual fantasies may enhance lovemaking.

M: ___a. Strongly agree ___ b. Agree ___c. Disagree ___d. Strongly disagree ___e. Let's discuss
F: ___a. Strongly agree ___ b. Agree ___c. Disagree ___d. Strongly disagree ___e. Let's discuss

285. Sexual fantasies are okay as long as people keep them to themselves.

M: ___a. Strongly agree ___ b. Agree ___c. Disagree ___d. Strongly disagree ___e. Let's discuss
F: ___a. Strongly agree ___ b. Agree ___c. Disagree ___d. Strongly disagree ___e. Let's discuss

286. Women do not have sexual fantasies.

M: ___a. Strongly agree ___ b. Agree ___c. Disagree ___d. Strongly disagree ___e. Let's discuss
F: ___a. Strongly agree ___ b. Agree ___c. Disagree ___d. Strongly disagree ___e. Let's discuss

287. Sexual fantasies are harmless *unless* they make one partner feel he or she is inadequate in some way.

M: ___a. Strongly agree ___ b. Agree ___c. Disagree ___d. Strongly disagree ___e. Let's discuss
F: ___a. Strongly agree ___ b. Agree ___c. Disagree ___d. Strongly disagree ___e. Let's discuss

288. It would bother me if my partner bought pornographic magazines, books, or videos.

M: ___a. Strongly agree ___ b. Agree ___c. Disagree ___d. Strongly disagree ___e. Let's discuss
F: ___a. Strongly agree ___ b. Agree ___c. Disagree ___d. Strongly disagree ___e. Let's discuss

289. I enjoy some types of pornographic magazines, books, and videos.

M: ___a. Strongly agree   ___ b. Agree   ___c. Disagree   ___d. Strongly disagree   ___e. Let's discuss
F: ___a. Strongly agree   ___ b. Agree   ___c. Disagree   ___d. Strongly disagree   ___e. Let's discuss

I don't have to say, "I love you" all the time! I let you drive my Camaro, don't I??

Romance. Say the word, and different people conjure up different images. Candlelight, soft music, flowers. Whispered words of love. Breakfast in bed. Giggles under the sheets.

Romance, to me, is exemplified by a couple, married fifty years — she still smiles at his jokes, and he tells her she is still the most beautiful woman in the world.

DIRECTIONS: **IF you are a male,** place your check mark next to the response that most closely matches how much you agree or disagree with each statement. Select "Let's discuss" *only* if you believe the other answers are not appropriate. Place your checkmark in the row opposite the "M," which stands for "male." **IF you are a female,** follow the same directions, except place your checkmark on the row marked "F" for "female."

290. Daily hugging and kissing are extremely important in a relationship.

M: ___a. Strongly agree ___b. Agree ___c. Disagree ___d. Strongly disagree ___e. Let's discuss
F: ___a. Strongly agree ___b. Agree ___c. Disagree ___d. Strongly disagree ___e. Let's discuss

291. I would feel hurt if my partner did not tell me "I love you" at least once a day.

M: ___a. Strongly agree ___b. Agree ___c. Disagree ___d. Strongly disagree ___e. Let's discuss
F: ___a. Strongly agree ___b. Agree ___c. Disagree ___d. Strongly disagree ___e. Let's discuss

292. If a man says he "wants some romance," he usually wants sex. If a woman says she "wants some romance," she usually wants loving attention and tenderness.

M: ___a. Strongly agree ___b. Agree ___c. Disagree ___d. Strongly disagree ___e. Let's discuss
F: ___a. Strongly agree ___b. Agree ___c. Disagree ___d. Strongly disagree ___e. Let's discuss

293. Flowers, candlelight dinners, and sweet little surprises may be clichés, but they are a vital part of keeping romance alive in a relationship.

M: ___a. Strongly agree ___ b. Agree ___c. Disagree ___d. Strongly disagree ___e. Let's discuss
F: ___a. Strongly agree ___ b. Agree ___c. Disagree ___d. Strongly disagree ___e. Let's discuss

294. My partner likes receiving flowers.

M: ___a. Strongly agree ___ b. Agree ___c. Disagree ___d. Strongly disagree ___e. Let's discuss
F: ___a. Strongly agree ___ b. Agree ___c. Disagree ___d. Strongly disagree ___e. Let's discuss

295. I like receiving flowers.

M: ___a. Strongly agree ___ b. Agree ___c. Disagree ___d. Strongly disagree ___e. Let's discuss
F: ___a. Strongly agree ___ b. Agree ___c. Disagree ___d. Strongly disagree ___e. Let's discuss

296. If you treat your partner with respect at all times, there is no need for any stereotypical "romantic" episodes.

M: ___a. Strongly agree ___ b. Agree ___c. Disagree ___d. Strongly disagree ___e. Let's discuss
F: ___a. Strongly agree ___ b. Agree ___c. Disagree ___d. Strongly disagree ___e. Let's discuss

297. Everybody needs a little romance once in a while.

M: ___a. Strongly agree ___ b. Agree ___c. Disagree ___d. Strongly disagree ___e. Let's discuss
F: ___a. Strongly agree ___ b. Agree ___c. Disagree ___d. Strongly disagree ___e. Let's discuss

298. Long, slow kisses are romantic.

M: ___a. Strongly agree ___ b. Agree ___c. Disagree ___d. Strongly disagree ___e. Let's discuss
F: ___a. Strongly agree ___ b. Agree ___c. Disagree ___d. Strongly disagree ___e. Let's discuss

299. If my partner sends me flowers after an argument, all is forgiven.

M: ___a. Strongly agree ___ b. Agree ___c. Disagree ___d. Strongly disagree ___e. Let's discuss
F: ___a. Strongly agree ___ b. Agree ___c. Disagree ___d. Strongly disagree ___e. Let's discuss

300. I enjoy receiving back massages.

M: ___a. Strongly agree ___ b. Agree ___c. Disagree ___d. Strongly disagree ___e. Let's discuss
F: ___a. Strongly agree ___ b. Agree ___c. Disagree ___d. Strongly disagree ___e. Let's discuss

301. I enjoy giving back massages.

M: ___a. Strongly agree ___ b. Agree ___c. Disagree ___d. Strongly disagree ___e. Let's discuss
F: ___a. Strongly agree ___ b. Agree ___c. Disagree ___d. Strongly disagree ___e. Let's discuss

302. If I wanted a back massage, and my partner refused to do it, I would be upset.

M: ___a. Strongly agree ___ b. Agree ___c. Disagree ___d. Strongly disagree ___e. Let's discuss
F: ___a. Strongly agree ___ b. Agree ___c. Disagree ___d. Strongly disagree ___e. Let's discuss

303. Displays of affection (kissing, holding hands) should be done only while in the home and not in public.

M: ___a. Strongly agree ___ b. Agree ___c. Disagree ___d. Strongly disagree ___e. Let's discuss
F: ___a. Strongly agree ___ b. Agree ___c. Disagree ___d. Strongly disagree ___e. Let's discuss

304. After a couple is married, it is not necessary to do romantic things that they did before they were married.

M: ___a. Strongly agree ___ b. Agree ___c. Disagree ___d. Strongly disagree ___e. Let's discuss
F: ___a. Strongly agree ___ b. Agree ___c. Disagree ___d. Strongly disagree ___e. Let's discuss

305. Love conquers all.

M: ___a. Strongly agree ___ b. Agree ___c. Disagree ___d. Strongly disagree ___e. Let's discuss
F: ___a. Strongly agree ___ b. Agree ___c. Disagree ___d. Strongly disagree ___e. Let's discuss

H.   Free Time

Leisure Activities

If you had a whole day to do anything you wanted, what would you do? Go for an early-morning jog and then go to a ball game in the afternoon? Or spend half the day at a bookstore or library and then attend a play in the evening? Would you expect your partner to join you in these activities? If your partner had other plans, how happy would you be to change yours?

DIRECTIONS: **IF you are a male,** place your check mark next to the response that most closely matches how much you agree or disagree with each statement. Select "Let's discuss" *only* if you believe the other answers are not appropriate. Place your checkmark in the row opposite the "M," which stands for "male." **IF you are a female,** follow the same directions, except place your checkmark on the row marked "F" for "female."

306. I don't have time for leisure activities.

M: ___a. Strongly agree ___ b. Agree ___c. Disagree ___d. Strongly disagree ___e. Let's discuss
F: ___a. Strongly agree ___ b. Agree ___c. Disagree ___d. Strongly disagree ___e. Let's discuss

307. I enjoy concerts.

M: ___a. Strongly agree ___ b. Agree ___c. Disagree ___d. Strongly disagree ___e. Let's discuss
F: ___a. Strongly agree ___ b. Agree ___c. Disagree ___d. Strongly disagree ___e. Let's discuss

308. I like to go out to dinner.

M: ___a. Strongly agree ___ b. Agree ___c. Disagree ___d. Strongly disagree ___e. Let's discuss
F: ___a. Strongly agree ___ b. Agree ___c. Disagree ___d. Strongly disagree ___e. Let's discuss

309. I don't mind spending money on hobbies I enjoy.

M: ___a. Strongly agree ___ b. Agree ___c. Disagree ___d. Strongly disagree ___e. Let's discuss
F: ___a. Strongly agree ___ b. Agree ___c. Disagree ___d. Strongly disagree ___e. Let's discuss

310. I enjoy my work so much that I prefer to work when I have any free time.

M: ___a. Strongly agree ___ b. Agree ___c. Disagree ___d. Strongly disagree ___e. Let's discuss
F: ___a. Strongly agree ___ b. Agree ___c. Disagree ___d. Strongly disagree ___e. Let's discuss

311. I like playing around on my computer.

M: ___a. Strongly agree ___ b. Agree ___c. Disagree ___d. Strongly disagree ___e. Let's discuss
F: ___a. Strongly agree ___ b. Agree ___c. Disagree ___d. Strongly disagree ___e. Let's discuss

312. I enjoy watching movies at movie theaters.

M: ___a. Strongly agree ___ b. Agree ___c. Disagree ___d. Strongly disagree ___e. Let's discuss
F: ___a. Strongly agree ___ b. Agree ___c. Disagree ___d. Strongly disagree ___e. Let's discuss

313. I don't like going out to the movies; it's much cheaper to rent a video.

M: ___a. Strongly agree ___ b. Agree ___c. Disagree ___d. Strongly disagree ___e. Let's discuss
F: ___a. Strongly agree ___ b. Agree ___c. Disagree ___d. Strongly disagree ___e. Let's discuss

314. I like to be punctual; I'm usually early to an event or social gathering.

M: ___a. Strongly agree ___ b. Agree ___c. Disagree ___d. Strongly disagree ___e. Let's discuss
F: ___a. Strongly agree ___ b. Agree ___c. Disagree ___d. Strongly disagree ___e. Let's discuss

315. People who are often late to events or social gatherings are rude.

M: ___a. Strongly agree ___ b. Agree ___c. Disagree ___d. Strongly disagree ___e. Let's discuss
F: ___a. Strongly agree ___ b. Agree ___c. Disagree ___d. Strongly disagree ___e. Let's discuss

316. I watch TV sports every week.

M: ___a. Strongly agree ___ b. Agree ___c. Disagree ___d. Strongly disagree ___e. Let's discuss
F: ___a. Strongly agree ___ b. Agree ___c. Disagree ___d. Strongly disagree ___e. Let's discuss

317. I enjoy attending sports events.

M: ___a. Strongly agree ___ b. Agree ___c. Disagree ___d. Strongly disagree ___e. Let's discuss
F: ___a. Strongly agree ___ b. Agree ___c. Disagree ___d. Strongly disagree ___e. Let's discuss

318. I enjoy participating in athletic events.

M: ___a. Strongly agree ___ b. Agree ___c. Disagree ___d. Strongly disagree ___e. Let's discuss
F: ___a. Strongly agree ___ b. Agree ___c. Disagree ___d. Strongly disagree ___e. Let's discuss

319. I expect my partner to participate in athletic events with me.

M: ___a. Strongly agree ___ b. Agree ___c. Disagree ___d. Strongly disagree ___e. Let's discuss
F: ___a. Strongly agree ___ b. Agree ___c. Disagree ___d. Strongly disagree ___e. Let's discuss

320. I like to listen to loud music.

M: ___a. Strongly agree ___ b. Agree ___c. Disagree ___d. Strongly disagree ___e. Let's discuss
F: ___a. Strongly agree ___ b. Agree ___c. Disagree ___d. Strongly disagree ___e. Let's discuss

321. I like clothes shopping.

M: ___a. Strongly agree ___ b. Agree ___c. Disagree ___d. Strongly disagree ___e. Let's discuss
F: ___a. Strongly agree ___ b. Agree ___c. Disagree ___d. Strongly disagree ___e. Let's discuss

322. I expect my partner to go clothes shopping with me.

M: ___a. Strongly agree ___ b. Agree ___c. Disagree ___d. Strongly disagree ___e. Let's discuss
F: ___a. Strongly agree ___ b. Agree ___c. Disagree ___d. Strongly disagree ___e. Let's discuss

323. I enjoy visiting "bed and breakfast" inns.

M: ___a. Strongly agree ___ b. Agree ___c. Disagree ___d. Strongly disagree ___e. Let's discuss
F: ___a. Strongly agree ___ b. Agree ___c. Disagree ___d. Strongly disagree ___e. Let's discuss

324. I like doing "touristy" things when I travel.

M: ___a. Strongly agree ___ b. Agree ___c. Disagree ___d. Strongly disagree ___e. Let's discuss
F: ___a. Strongly agree ___ b. Agree ___c. Disagree ___d. Strongly disagree ___e. Let's discuss

325. I prefer to stay in a hotel, rather than go camping, during my vacations.

M: ___a. Strongly agree ___ b. Agree ___ c. Disagree ___d. Strongly disagree ___e. Let's discuss
F: ___a. Strongly agree ___ b. Agree ___ c. Disagree ___d. Strongly disagree ___e. Let's discuss

326. I like to get as far away from people as I possibly can when I go on vacation.

M: ___a. Strongly agree ___ b. Agree ___ c. Disagree ___d. Strongly disagree ___e. Let's discuss
F: ___a. Strongly agree ___ b. Agree ___ c. Disagree ___d. Strongly disagree ___e. Let's discuss

327. I like gambling.

M: ___a. Strongly agree ___ b. Agree ___ c. Disagree ___d. Strongly disagree ___e. Let's discuss
F: ___a. Strongly agree ___ b. Agree ___ c. Disagree ___d. Strongly disagree ___e. Let's discuss

328. I set aside money to gamble every week.

M: ___a. Strongly agree ___ b. Agree ___ c. Disagree ___d. Strongly disagree ___e. Let's discuss
F: ___a. Strongly agree ___ b. Agree ___ c. Disagree ___d. Strongly disagree ___e. Let's discuss

329. I may spend a lot of money gambling, but I win most of it back.

M: ___a. Strongly agree ___ b. Agree ___ c. Disagree ___d. Strongly disagree ___e. Let's discuss
F: ___a. Strongly agree ___ b. Agree ___ c. Disagree ___d. Strongly disagree ___e. Let's discuss

330. I like RV (recreational vehicle) camping.

M: ___a. Strongly agree ___ b. Agree ___ c. Disagree ___d. Strongly disagree ___e. Let's discuss
F: ___a. Strongly agree ___ b. Agree ___ c. Disagree ___d. Strongly disagree ___e. Let's discuss

331. I enjoy fishing and boating.

M: ___a. Strongly agree ___ b. Agree ___ c. Disagree ___d. Strongly disagree ___e. Let's discuss
F: ___a. Strongly agree ___ b. Agree ___ c. Disagree ___d. Strongly disagree ___e. Let's discuss

332. I enjoy going to museums.

M: ___a. Strongly agree ___ b. Agree ___ c. Disagree ___d. Strongly disagree ___e. Let's discuss
F: ___a. Strongly agree ___ b. Agree ___ c. Disagree ___d. Strongly disagree ___e. Let's discuss

333. I expect my partner to share all my interests.

M: ___a. Strongly agree ___ b. Agree ___c. Disagree ___d. Strongly disagree ___e. Let's discuss
F: ___a. Strongly agree ___ b. Agree ___c. Disagree ___d. Strongly disagree ___e. Let's discuss

334. During vacations, I enjoy staying home.

M: ___a. Strongly agree ___ b. Agree ___c. Disagree ___d. Strongly disagree ___e. Let's discuss
F: ___a. Strongly agree ___ b. Agree ___c. Disagree ___d. Strongly disagree ___e. Let's discuss

335. I enjoy traveling.

M: ___a. Strongly agree ___ b. Agree ___c. Disagree ___d. Strongly disagree ___e. Let's discuss
F: ___a. Strongly agree ___ b. Agree ___c. Disagree ___d. Strongly disagree ___e. Let's discuss

336. I would rather stay home in peace and quiet than go to a crowded public event.

M: ___a. Strongly agree ___ b. Agree ___c. Disagree ___d. Strongly disagree ___e. Let's discuss
F: ___a. Strongly agree ___ b. Agree ___c. Disagree ___d. Strongly disagree ___e. Let's discuss

337. I watch television at least three hours each day.

M: ___a. Strongly agree ___ b. Agree ___c. Disagree ___d. Strongly disagree ___e. Let's discuss
F: ___a. Strongly agree ___ b. Agree ___c. Disagree ___d. Strongly disagree ___e. Let's discuss

338. I believe it is healthy and acceptable if my partner and I each wish to pursue our own separate interests.

M. ___a. Strongly agree ___ b. Agree ___c. Disagree ___d. Strongly disagree ___e. Let's discuss
F: ___a. Strongly agree ___ b. Agree ___c. Disagree ___d. Strongly disagree ___e. Let's discuss

Holidays

Do you enjoy holidays? Do you love the sights and sounds — from July fireworks and Christmas carols to Halloween pranks and Thanksgiving dinners? Or do you think the best holiday activity would be to spend a week with your partner on a tropical island, far from the rest of the world?

DIRECTIONS: **IF you are a male,** place your check mark next to the response that most closely matches how much you agree or disagree with each statement. Select "Let's discuss" *only* if you believe the other answers are not appropriate. Place your checkmark in the row opposite the "M," which stands for "male." **IF you are a female,** follow the same directions, except place your checkmark on the row marked "F" for "female."

339. I enjoy celebrating holidays.

M:　　___a. Strongly agree ___ b. Agree ___c. Disagree ___d. Strongly disagree ___e. Let's discuss
F:　　___a. Strongly agree ___ b. Agree ___c. Disagree ___d. Strongly disagree ___e. Let's discuss

340. I enjoy celebrating anniversaries.

M:　　___a. Strongly agree ___ b. Agree ___c. Disagree ___d. Strongly disagree ___e. Let's discuss
F:　　___a. Strongly agree ___ b. Agree ___c. Disagree ___d. Strongly disagree ___e. Let's discuss

341. I will always celebrate the holidays of my religion.

M:　　___a. Strongly agree ___ b. Agree ___c. Disagree ___d. Strongly disagree ___e. Let's discuss
F:　　___a. Strongly agree ___ b. Agree ___c. Disagree ___d. Strongly disagree ___e. Let's discuss

342. I do not currently celebrate the holidays of my religion, but I would like to do so in the future.

M:　　___a. Strongly agree ___ b. Agree ___c. Disagree ___d. Strongly disagree ___e. Let's discuss
F:　　___a. Strongly agree ___ b. Agree ___c. Disagree ___d. Strongly disagree ___e. Let's discuss

343. I would be very unhappy if my partner forgot my birthday or an anniversary.

M: ___a. Strongly agree ___ b. Agree ___c. Disagree ___d. Strongly disagree ___e. Let's discuss
F: ___a. Strongly agree ___ b. Agree ___c. Disagree ___d. Strongly disagree ___e. Let's discuss

344. I believe it is important to put aside money throughout the year in order to purchase high-quality gifts during the winter holidays.

M: ___a. Strongly agree ___ b. Agree ___c. Disagree ___d. Strongly disagree ___e. Let's discuss
F: ___a. Strongly agree ___ b. Agree ___c. Disagree ___d. Strongly disagree ___e. Let's discuss

345. I think people spend too much money on holiday gifts.

M: ___a. Strongly agree ___ b. Agree ___c. Disagree ___d. Strongly disagree ___e. Let's discuss
F: ___a. Strongly agree ___ b. Agree ___c. Disagree ___d. Strongly disagree ___e. Let's discuss

346. I enjoy giving people expensive gifts.

M: ___a. Strongly agree ___ b. Agree ___c. Disagree ___d. Strongly disagree ___e. Let's discuss
F: ___a. Strongly agree ___ b. Agree ___c. Disagree ___d. Strongly disagree ___e. Let's discuss

347. I enjoy giving people gifts, not necessarily expensive gifts.

M: ___a. Strongly agree ___ b. Agree ___c. Disagree ___d. Strongly disagree ___e. Let's discuss
F: ___a. Strongly agree ___ b. Agree ___c. Disagree ___d. Strongly disagree ___e. Let's discuss

348. I would be very sad if my partner did not remember me with flowers, candy, or at least a card on St. Valentine's Day.

M: ___a. Strongly agree ___ b. Agree ___c. Disagree ___d. Strongly disagree ___e. Let's discuss
F: ___a. Strongly agree ___ b. Agree ___c. Disagree ___d. Strongly disagree ___e. Let's discuss

349. I have always spent the winter holidays with my parent(s), and would not consider other options.

M: ___a. Strongly agree ___ b. Agree ___c. Disagree ___d. Strongly disagree ___e. Let's discuss
F: ___a. Strongly agree ___ b. Agree ___c. Disagree ___d. Strongly disagree ___e. Let's discuss

350. I would be unhappy if my partner gave me a low-cost holiday present.

M: ___a. Strongly agree ___ b. Agree ___c. Disagree ___d. Strongly disagree ___e. Let's discuss
F: ___a. Strongly agree ___ b. Agree ___c. Disagree ___d. Strongly disagree ___e. Let's discuss

351. The cost of a present is not important; the thought behind it is what is important.

M: ___a. Strongly agree ___ b. Agree ___c. Disagree ___d. Strongly disagree ___e. Let's discuss
F: ___a. Strongly agree ___ b. Agree ___c. Disagree ___d. Strongly disagree ___e. Let's discuss

352. I would be unhappy if my partner gave me a present that did not match any of my needs or preferences, indicating he or she did not put much thought into selecting it.

M: ___a. Strongly agree ___ b. Agree ___c. Disagree ___d. Strongly disagree ___e. Let's discuss
F: ___a. Strongly agree ___ b. Agree ___c. Disagree ___d. Strongly disagree ___e. Let's discuss

353. Gifts of kindness and loving deeds have more value than material gifts.

M: ___a. Strongly agree ___ b. Agree ___c. Disagree ___d. Strongly disagree ___e. Let's discuss
F: ___a. Strongly agree ___ b. Agree ___c. Disagree ___d. Strongly disagree ___e. Let's discuss

354. The holidays are a great time to buy a nice gift for your partner to express appreciation for the gifts of kindness and loving deeds he or she gave you throughout the year.

M: ___a. Strongly agree ___ b. Agree ___c. Disagree ___d. Strongly disagree ___e. Let's discuss
F: ___a. Strongly agree ___ b. Agree ___c. Disagree ___d. Strongly disagree ___e. Let's discuss

Cars

What are your thoughts on the driving machine in your life? For some people, a good car is one that carries them from one place to another without breaking down. For others, it is the latest model in the flashiest color. What about you?

DIRECTIONS: **IF you are a male,** place your check mark next to the response that most closely matches how much you agree or disagree with each statement. Select "Let's discuss" *only* if you believe the other answers are not appropriate. Place your checkmark in the row opposite the "M," which stands for "male." **IF you are a female,** follow the same directions, except place your checkmark on the row marked "F" for "female."

355. It is important to me to drive a nice, relatively new car.

M: ___a. Strongly agree ___b. Agree ___c. Disagree ___d. Strongly disagree ___e. Let's discuss
F: ___a. Strongly agree ___b. Agree ___c. Disagree ___d. Strongly disagree ___e. Let's discuss

356. I think it's important to buy the best car that you can possibly afford.

M: ___a. Strongly agree ___b. Agree ___c. Disagree ___d. Strongly disagree ___e. Let's discuss
F: ___a. Strongly agree ___b. Agree ___c. Disagree ___d. Strongly disagree ___e. Let's discuss

357. I would be embarrassed to be seen riding in or driving an old rusty car.

M: ___a. Strongly agree ___b. Agree ___c. Disagree ___d. Strongly disagree ___e. Let's discuss
F: ___a. Strongly agree ___b. Agree ___c. Disagree ___d. Strongly disagree ___e. Let's discuss

358. I try to buy a new car every two years or so.

M: ___a. Strongly agree ___b. Agree ___c. Disagree ___d. Strongly disagree ___e. Let's discuss
F: ___a. Strongly agree ___b. Agree ___c. Disagree ___d. Strongly disagree ___e. Let's discuss

359. I like to fix cars.

M: ___a. Strongly agree ___b. Agree ___c. Disagree ___d. Strongly disagree ___e. Let's discuss
F: ___a. Strongly agree ___b. Agree ___c. Disagree ___d. Strongly disagree ___e. Let's discuss

360. The make and model of a car are not important to me; it's important if the car is dependable.

M: ___a. Strongly agree ___ b. Agree ___c. Disagree ___d. Strongly disagree ___e. Let's discuss
F: ___a. Strongly agree ___ b. Agree ___c. Disagree ___d. Strongly disagree ___e. Let's discuss

361. I always buckle my seat belt.

M: ___a. Strongly agree ___ b. Agree ___c. Disagree ___d. Strongly disagree ___e. Let's discuss
F: ___a. Strongly agree ___ b. Agree ___c. Disagree ___d. Strongly disagree ___e. Let's discuss

362. It is important to keep the interior and exterior of your vehicle clean at all times.

M: ___a. Strongly agree ___ b. Agree ___c. Disagree ___d. Strongly disagree ___e. Let's discuss
F: ___a. Strongly agree ___ b. Agree ___c. Disagree ___d. Strongly disagree ___e. Let's discuss

363. I like pickup trucks.

M: ___a. Strongly agree ___ b. Agree ___c. Disagree ___d. Strongly disagree ___e. Let's discuss
F: ___a. Strongly agree ___ b. Agree ___c. Disagree ___d. Strongly disagree ___e. Let's discuss

364. I like motorcycles.

M: ___a. Strongly agree ___ b. Agree ___c. Disagree ___d. Strongly disagree ___e. Let's discuss
F: ___a. Strongly agree ___ b. Agree ___c. Disagree ___d. Strongly disagree ___e. Let's discuss

Pets

Are you a cat person? Do you ignore the cat hair in your food as well as cheerfully replace your scratched-up furniture, drapes, and wallpaper on a regular basis? Or do you prefer to put up with fleas, chewed shoes, and occasional soiled carpets in exchange for the love of a favorite mutt?

Complete the following questions to see if you and your partner are pet-compatible!

Pets

DIRECTIONS: **IF you are a male,** place your check mark next to the response that most closely matches how much you agree or disagree with each statement. Select "Let's discuss" *only* if you believe the other answers are not appropriate. Place your checkmark in the row opposite the "M," which stands for "male." **IF you are a female,** follow the same directions, except place your checkmark on the row marked "F" for "female."

365. In general, I like most pets.

M: ___a. Strongly agree ___ b. Agree ___c. Disagree ___d. Strongly disagree ___e. Let's discuss
F: ___a. Strongly agree ___ b. Agree ___c. Disagree ___d. Strongly disagree ___e. Let's discuss

366. I like dogs as pets.

M: ___a. Strongly agree ___ b. Agree ___c. Disagree ___d. Strongly disagree ___e. Let's discuss
F: ___a. Strongly agree ___ b. Agree ___c. Disagree ___d. Strongly disagree ___e. Let's discuss

367. I like cats as pets.

M: ___a. Strongly agree ___ b. Agree ___c. Disagree ___d. Strongly disagree ___e. Let's discuss
F: ___a. Strongly agree ___ b. Agree ___c. Disagree ___d. Strongly disagree ___e. Let's discuss

368. It would bother me to see a cat sleeping on a kitchen or dining room table.

M: ___a. Strongly agree ___ b. Agree ___c. Disagree ___d. Strongly disagree ___e. Let's discuss
F: ___a. Strongly agree ___ b. Agree ___c. Disagree ___d. Strongly disagree ___e. Let's discuss

369. It bothers me when dogs jump up on me when I visit friends' homes.

M: ___a. Strongly agree ___ b. Agree ___c. Disagree ___d. Strongly disagree ___e. Let's discuss
F: ___a. Strongly agree ___ b. Agree ___c. Disagree ___d. Strongly disagree ___e. Let's discuss

370. It bothers me when I see someone place a dinner dish on the floor so a dog or cat can finish the scraps.

M: ___a. Strongly agree ___ b. Agree ___c. Disagree ___d. Strongly disagree ___e. Let's discuss
F: ___a. Strongly agree ___ b. Agree ___c. Disagree ___d. Strongly disagree ___e. Let's discuss

371. I am allergic to cats and/or other animals.

M: ___a. Strongly agree ___ b. Agree ___c. Disagree ___d. Strongly disagree ___e. Let's discuss
F: ___a. Strongly agree ___ b. Agree ___c. Disagree ___d. Strongly disagree ___e. Let's discuss

372. My child is allergic to cats and/or other animals.

M: ___a. Strongly agree ___ b. Agree ___c. Disagree ___d. Strongly disagree ___e. Let's discuss
F: ___a. Strongly agree ___ b. Agree ___c. Disagree ___d. Strongly disagree ___e. Let's discuss

373. I think the homes of people who have cats have a distinct and unpleasant odor.

M: ___a. Strongly agree ___ b. Agree ___c. Disagree ___d. Strongly disagree ___e. Let's discuss
F: ___a. Strongly agree ___ b. Agree ___c. Disagree ___d. Strongly disagree ___e. Let's discuss

374. I think the homes of people who have dogs have a distinct and unpleasant odor.

M: ___a. Strongly agree ___ b. Agree ___c. Disagree ___d. Strongly disagree ___e. Let's discuss
F: ___a. Strongly agree ___ b. Agree ___c. Disagree ___d. Strongly disagree ___e. Let's discuss

375. I would never own a dog that regularly drooled.

M: ___a. Strongly agree ___ b. Agree ___c. Disagree ___d. Strongly disagree ___e. Let's discuss
F: ___a. Strongly agree ___ b. Agree ___c. Disagree ___d. Strongly disagree ___e. Let's discuss

376. It would not bother me if my partner kept rodents as pets.

M: ___a. Strongly agree ___ b. Agree ___c. Disagree ___d. Strongly disagree ___e. Let's discuss
F: ___a. Strongly agree ___ b. Agree ___c. Disagree ___d. Strongly disagree ___e. Let's discuss

377. The squawking of pet birds does not bother me.

M: ___a. Strongly agree ___ b. Agree ___c. Disagree ___d. Strongly disagree ___e. Let's discuss
F: ___a. Strongly agree ___ b. Agree ___c. Disagree ___d. Strongly disagree ___e. Let's discuss

378. I like reptiles as pets.

M: ___a. Strongly agree ___ b. Agree ___c. Disagree ___d. Strongly disagree ___e. Let's discuss
F: ___a. Strongly agree ___ b. Agree ___c. Disagree ___d. Strongly disagree ___e. Let's discuss

379. I like birds as pets.

M: ___a. Strongly agree ___ b. Agree ___c. Disagree ___d. Strongly disagree ___e. Let's discuss
F: ___a. Strongly agree ___ b. Agree ___c. Disagree ___d. Strongly disagree ___e. Let's discuss

380. I like fish as pets.

M: ___a. Strongly agree ___ b. Agree ___c. Disagree ___d. Strongly disagree ___e. Let's discuss
F: ___a. Strongly agree ___ b. Agree ___c. Disagree ___d. Strongly disagree ___e. Let's discuss

381. I would prefer not to have any pets.

M: ___a. Strongly agree ___ b. Agree ___c. Disagree ___d. Strongly disagree ___e. Let's discuss
F: ___a. Strongly agree ___ b. Agree ___c. Disagree ___d. Strongly disagree ___e. Let's discuss

Look! Eldon likes you! He really likes you!"

I. Miscellaneous: Passing Gas, Burping, and Body Odor

Does your partner pass gas, burp, or reek of perspiration? I know several women who have suffered in such relationships.

It is common knowledge that *women do not pass gas*. Ask anyone. This section is included for the benefit of those women contemplating marriage so they can plan for their future domestic bliss — perhaps by requesting nose plugs, air filtration systems, white noise machines, and men's toiletries as shower gifts.

382. If someone loves you, that person should be able to tolerate it when you have to pass gas.

M: ___a. Strongly agree ___ b. Agree ___c. Disagree ___d. Strongly disagree ___e. Let's discuss
F: ___a. Strongly agree ___ b. Agree ___c. Disagree ___d. Strongly disagree ___e. Let's discuss

383. Passing gas is healthy and normal and should never be suppressed.

M: ___a. Strongly agree ___ b. Agree ___c. Disagree ___d. Strongly disagree ___e. Let's discuss
F: ___a. Strongly agree ___ b. Agree ___c. Disagree ___d. Strongly disagree ___e. Let's discuss

384. It's rude to pass gas in front of other people, especially one's partner.

M: ___a. Strongly agree ___ b. Agree ___c. Disagree ___d. Strongly disagree ___e. Let's discuss
F: ___a. Strongly agree ___ b. Agree ___c. Disagree ___d. Strongly disagree ___e. Let's discuss

385. If you pass gas, you should leave the room; if that is not possible, you should just pretend it didn't happen.

M: ___a. Strongly agree ___ b. Agree ___c. Disagree ___d. Strongly disagree ___e. Let's discuss
F: ___a. Strongly agree ___ b. Agree ___c. Disagree ___d. Strongly disagree ___e. Let's discuss

386. If you think someone *knows* you passed gas, you should always say, "Excuse me."

M: ___a. Strongly agree ___ b. Agree ___c. Disagree ___d. Strongly disagree ___e. Let's discuss
F: ___a. Strongly agree ___ b. Agree ___c. Disagree ___d. Strongly disagree ___e. Let's discuss

387. It's okay to pass gas in your own home, no matter who is in the room.

M: ___a. Strongly agree ___ b. Agree ___c. Disagree ___d. Strongly disagree ___e. Let's discuss
F: ___a. Strongly agree ___ b. Agree ___c. Disagree ___d. Strongly disagree ___e. Let's discuss

388. People who ask you to pull their finger just before they pass gas should be jailed with no parole.

M: ___a. Strongly agree ___ b. Agree ___c. Disagree ___d. Strongly disagree ___e. Let's discuss
F: ___a. Strongly agree ___ b. Agree ___c. Disagree ___d. Strongly disagree ___e. Let's discuss

389. It is immature to discuss passed gas.

M: ___a. Strongly agree ___ b. Agree ___c. Disagree ___d. Strongly disagree ___e. Let's discuss
F: ___a. Strongly agree ___ b. Agree ___c. Disagree ___d. Strongly disagree ___e. Let's discuss

390. It is rude to burp in front of others.

M: ___a. Strongly agree ___ b. Agree ___c. Disagree ___d. Strongly disagree ___e. Let's discuss
F: ___a. Strongly agree ___ b. Agree ___c. Disagree ___d. Strongly disagree ___e. Let's discuss

391. It is rude to burp in front of one's partner.

M: ___a. Strongly agree ___ b. Agree ___c. Disagree ___d. Strongly disagree ___e. Let's discuss
F: ___a. Strongly agree ___ b. Agree ___c. Disagree ___d. Strongly disagree ___e. Let's discuss

392. Burping is healthy and normal and should not be suppressed at any time.

M: ___a. Strongly agree ___ b. Agree ___c. Disagree ___d. Strongly disagree ___e. Let's discuss
F: ___a. Strongly agree ___ b. Agree ___c. Disagree ___d. Strongly disagree ___e. Let's discuss

393. If you have to burp, you should always say, "Excuse me."

M: ___a. Strongly agree ___ b. Agree ___c. Disagree ___d. Strongly disagree ___e. Let's discuss
F: ___a. Strongly agree ___ b. Agree ___c. Disagree ___d. Strongly disagree ___e. Let's discuss

Miscellaneous

394. If you need to burp or pass gas, you should immediately run into the nearest bathroom or public washroom.

M: ___a. Strongly agree ___ b. Agree ___c. Disagree ___d. Strongly disagree ___e. Let's discuss
F: ___a. Strongly agree ___ b. Agree ___c. Disagree ___d. Strongly disagree ___e. Let's discuss

395. Body odor is normal and natural and should not be disguised with perfumes and deodorants.

M: ___a. Strongly agree ___ b. Agree ___c. Disagree ___d. Strongly disagree ___e. Let's discuss
F: ___a. Strongly agree ___ b. Agree ___c. Disagree ___d. Strongly disagree ___e. Let's discuss

396. Daily showers or baths are a necessity for both men and women.

M: ___a. Strongly agree ___ b. Agree ___c. Disagree ___d. Strongly disagree ___e. Let's discuss
F: ___a. Strongly agree ___ b. Agree ___c. Disagree ___d. Strongly disagree ___e. Let's discuss

397. If my partner did not use anti-perspirant and deodorant, I would end our relationship.

M: ___a. Strongly agree ___ b. Agree ___c. Disagree ___d. Strongly disagree ___e. Let's discuss
F: ___a. Strongly agree ___ b. Agree ___c. Disagree ___d. Strongly disagree ___e. Let's discuss

398. If you sneeze, you should always make sure you sneeze into a tissue or handkerchief, and _never_ a cloth napkin at a dinner table.

M: ___a. Strongly agree ___ b. Agree ___c. Disagree ___d. Strongly disagree ___e. Let's discuss
F: ___a. Strongly agree ___ b. Agree ___c. Disagree ___d. Strongly disagree ___e. Let's discuss

399. If anyone sneezes near you, you should _always_ say, "God bless you."

M: ___a. Strongly agree ___ b. Agree ___c. Disagree ___d. Strongly disagree ___e. Let's discuss
F: ___a. Strongly agree ___ b. Agree ___c. Disagree ___d. Strongly disagree ___e. Let's discuss

Raymond, stop blaming your farts on the dog! Rocky died three years ago.

II. THE GREAT DEBATES: COMMONLY ARGUED TOPICS

Imagine the home of Mr. and Mrs. Eversohappi. They never fight. Never, never, never. They agree on *everything*. They sit on their beautiful raspberry/cream floral couch (the one in which they totally agreed upon its price, color, and style), in front of their television (the one in which they totally agreed upon its price, size and style) and watch a program (a PBS special on iguanas upon which they totally agreed to watch). They are ever, *ever* so *happy*! (Yeah, *right*.)

There are *so many things* for a couple to argue about; and so little time. I say don't waste your time on the little things! Aim high! Shoot for the biggies: money, household duties, relatives, and kids!

Seriously — it's a good idea to discuss these issues before they become huge, overwhelming roadblocks on your road to happiness. This section covers those biggies.

Money

Money is the biggest of the "biggies." It's a common topic of discussion in *many* homes throughout the United States, and probably Canada and Mexico, too. Perhaps some people are simply genetically predisposed to overspending and creatively justifying their purchases. Yeah, that's it. *Genetics*.

What about you? Do you think you should spend as much as possible now, since, as we all know, you can't take it with you? Or do you enjoy saving for a rainy day...or for the mortgage payment?

DIRECTIONS: **IF you are a male,** place your check mark next to the response that most closely matches how much you agree or disagree with each statement. Select "Let's discuss" *only* if you believe the other answers are not appropriate. Place your checkmark in the row opposite the "M," which stands for "male." **IF you are a female,** follow the same directions, except place your checkmark on the row marked "F" for "female."

400. When two people date, the man should pay all expenses.

M: ___a. Strongly agree ___ b. Agree ___c. Disagree ___d. Strongly disagree ___e. Let's discuss
F: ___a. Strongly agree ___ b. Agree ___c. Disagree ___d. Strongly disagree ___e. Let's discuss

401. A married couple should keep all expenses separate and determine who will pay for each expense.

M: ___a. Strongly agree ___ b. Agree ___c. Disagree ___d. Strongly disagree ___e. Let's discuss
F: ___a. Strongly agree ___ b. Agree ___c. Disagree ___d. Strongly disagree ___e. Let's discuss

402. A married couple should combine 100% of the money they earn and pay all expenses from that amount.

M: ___a. Strongly agree ___ b. Agree ___c. Disagree ___d. Strongly disagree ___e. Let's discuss
F: ___a. Strongly agree ___ b. Agree ___c. Disagree ___d. Strongly disagree ___e. Let's discuss

403. Married couples should have separate *checking* accounts.

M: ___a. Strongly agree ___ b. Agree ___c. Disagree ___d. Strongly disagree ___e. Let's discuss
F: ___a. Strongly agree ___ b. Agree ___c. Disagree ___d. Strongly disagree ___e. Let's discuss

404. Married couples should have separate *savings* accounts.

M: ___a. Strongly agree ___ b. Agree ___c. Disagree ___d. Strongly disagree ___e. Let's discuss
F: ___a. Strongly agree ___ b. Agree ___c. Disagree ___d. Strongly disagree ___e. Let's discuss

405. The husband should handle the finances.

M: ___a. Strongly agree ___ b. Agree ___c. Disagree ___d. Strongly disagree ___e. Let's discuss
F: ___a. Strongly agree ___ b. Agree ___c. Disagree ___d. Strongly disagree ___e. Let's discuss

406. The wife should handle the finances.

M: ___a. Strongly agree ___ b. Agree ___c. Disagree ___d. Strongly disagree ___e. Let's discuss
F: ___a. Strongly agree ___ b. Agree ___c. Disagree ___d. Strongly disagree ___e. Let's discuss

407. A husband and wife should handle the finances together, with equal responsibility and decision-making roles.

M: ___a. Strongly agree ___ b. Agree ___c. Disagree ___d. Strongly disagree ___e. Let's discuss
F: ___a. Strongly agree ___ b. Agree ___c. Disagree ___d. Strongly disagree ___e. Let's discuss

408. One spouse should get an allowance and the other person should handle the finances.

M: ___a. Strongly agree ___ b. Agree ___c. Disagree ___d. Strongly disagree ___e. Let's discuss
F: ___a. Strongly agree ___ b. Agree ___c. Disagree ___d. Strongly disagree ___e. Let's discuss

409. A formal budget is the best way to handle finances.

M: ___a. Strongly agree ___ b. Agree ___c. Disagree ___d. Strongly disagree ___e. Let's discuss
F: ___a. Strongly agree ___ b. Agree ___c. Disagree ___d. Strongly disagree ___e. Let's discuss

410. I balance my checkbook every month.

M: ___a. Strongly agree ___ b. Agree ___c. Disagree ___d. Strongly disagree ___e. Let's discuss
F: ___a. Strongly agree ___ b. Agree ___c. Disagree ___d. Strongly disagree ___e. Let's discuss

Money

411. I never balance my checkbook.

M: ___a. Strongly agree ___ b. Agree ___c. Disagree ___d. Strongly disagree ___e. Let's discuss
F: ___a. Strongly agree ___ b. Agree ___c. Disagree ___d. Strongly disagree ___e. Let's discuss

412. I think it is okay to charge purchases up to the limit of the charge card and carry the balances month to month.

M: ___a. Strongly agree ___ b. Agree ___c. Disagree ___d. Strongly disagree ___e. Let's discuss
F: ___a. Strongly agree ___ b. Agree ___c. Disagree ___d. Strongly disagree ___e. Let's discuss

413. I think it's important to pay off balances each month on charge cards.

M: ___a. Strongly agree ___ b. Agree ___c. Disagree ___d. Strongly disagree ___e. Let's discuss
F: ___a. Strongly agree ___ b. Agree ___c. Disagree ___d. Strongly disagree ___e. Let's discuss

414. It is important to save in order to enjoy things, such as vacation travel.

M: ___a. Strongly agree ___ b. Agree ___c. Disagree ___d. Strongly disagree ___e. Let's discuss
F: ___a. Strongly agree ___ b. Agree ___c. Disagree ___d. Strongly disagree ___e. Let's discuss

415. If I want to do something, such as take a trip, I have no qualms about charging it to a credit card.

M: ___a. Strongly agree ___ b. Agree ___c. Disagree ___d. Strongly disagree ___e. Let's discuss
F: ___a. Strongly agree ___ b. Agree ___c. Disagree ___d. Strongly disagree ___e. Let's discuss

416. I save part of every paycheck.

M: ___a. Strongly agree ___ b. Agree ___c. Disagree ___d. Strongly disagree ___e. Let's discuss
F: ___a. Strongly agree ___ b. Agree ___c. Disagree ___d. Strongly disagree ___e. Let's discuss

417. If I were to marry, I would expect my spouse to sign a prenuptial agreement.

M: ___a. Strongly agree ___ b. Agree ___c. Disagree ___d. Strongly disagree ___e. Let's discuss
F: ___a. Strongly agree ___ b. Agree ___c. Disagree ___d. Strongly disagree ___e. Let's discuss

418. **If I were to marry, and my spouse had large debts, I would agree to pay off those debts.**

M: ___a. Strongly agree ___ b. Agree ___c. Disagree ___d. Strongly disagree ___e. Let's discuss
F: ___a. Strongly agree ___ b. Agree ___c. Disagree ___d. Strongly disagree ___e. Let's discuss

419. **If I were to marry, I would expect my spouse to independently pay off any debts he or she incurred before our marriage.**

M: ___a. Strongly agree ___ b. Agree ___c. Disagree ___d. Strongly disagree ___e. Let's discuss
F: ___a. Strongly agree ___ b. Agree ___c. Disagree ___d. Strongly disagree ___e. Let's discuss

420. **If I were to marry, and my spouse bought more things than we could afford and created large debts, I would be very angry (because legally I would be responsible for those debts if they were created with joint credit).**

M: ___a. Strongly agree ___ b. Agree ___c. Disagree ___d. Strongly disagree ___e. Let's discuss
F: ___a. Strongly agree ___ b. Agree ___c. Disagree ___d. Strongly disagree ___e. Let's discuss

421. **If only one spouse is working (outside the home) in a marriage, the working spouse should control where the money goes.**

M: ___a. Strongly agree ___ b. Agree ___c. Disagree ___d. Strongly disagree ___e. Let's discuss
F: ___a. Strongly agree ___ b. Agree ___c. Disagree ___d. Strongly disagree ___e. Let's discuss

422. **A married couple should make *all* purchases by joint decision.**

M: ___a. Strongly agree ___ b. Agree ___c. Disagree ___d. Strongly disagree ___e. Let's discuss
F: ___a. Strongly agree ___ b. Agree ___c. Disagree ___d. Strongly disagree ___e. Let's discuss

423. **A married couple should make only *major* purchases by joint decision.**

M: ___a. Strongly agree ___ b. Agree ___c. Disagree ___d. Strongly disagree ___e. Let's discuss
F: ___a. Strongly agree ___ b. Agree ___c. Disagree ___d. Strongly disagree ___e. Let's discuss

424. If I were married, and my spouse needed a new car, I would expect my spouse to pay for all of it if he/she were working.

M: ___ a. Strongly agree ___ b. Agree ___ c. Disagree ___ d. Strongly disagree ___ e. Let's discuss
F: ___ a. Strongly agree ___ b. Agree ___ c. Disagree ___ d. Strongly disagree ___ e. Let's discuss

425. If my spouse wanted to quit work to continue school full time, I would have no objection to supporting him/her.

M: ___ a. Strongly agree ___ b. Agree ___ c. Disagree ___ d. Strongly disagree ___ e. Let's discuss
F: ___ a. Strongly agree ___ b. Agree ___ c. Disagree ___ d. Strongly disagree ___ e. Let's discuss

426. If I wanted to quit work to continue schooling full time, I would expect my spouse to support me financially.

M: ___ a. Strongly agree ___ b. Agree ___ c. Disagree ___ d. Strongly disagree ___ e. Let's discuss
F: ___ a. Strongly agree ___ b. Agree ___ c. Disagree ___ d. Strongly disagree ___ e. Let's discuss

427. The spouse earning the higher income should make the major financial decisions.

M: ___ a. Strongly agree ___ b. Agree ___ c. Disagree ___ d. Strongly disagree ___ e. Let's discuss
F: ___ a. Strongly agree ___ b. Agree ___ c. Disagree ___ d. Strongly disagree ___ e. Let's discuss

428. The spouse earning the higher income should not be expected to handle as many of the household chores as the spouse with a lower income.

M: ___ a. Strongly agree ___ b. Agree ___ c. Disagree ___ d. Strongly disagree ___ e. Let's discuss
F: ___ a. Strongly agree ___ b. Agree ___ c. Disagree ___ d. Strongly disagree ___ e. Let's discuss

429. The spouse with the most important job is the person who earns the higher income.

M: ___ a. Strongly agree ___ b. Agree ___ c. Disagree ___ d. Strongly disagree ___ e. Let's discuss
F: ___ a. Strongly agree ___ b. Agree ___ c. Disagree ___ d. Strongly disagree ___ e. Let's discuss

430. **The spouse who earns the higher income is often more physically exhausted at the end of the day than the spouse who earns the lower (or no) income.**

M: ___a. Strongly agree ___b. Agree ___c. Disagree ___d. Strongly disagree ___e. Let's discuss
F: ___a. Strongly agree ___b. Agree ___c. Disagree ___d. Strongly disagree ___e. Let's discuss

431. **If my spouse's relative(s) needed money (and could not afford to repay a loan), I would have no problem giving them money and not expect repayment.**

M: ___a. Strongly agree ___b. Agree ___c. Disagree ___d. Strongly disagree ___e. Let's discuss
F: ___a. Strongly agree ___b. Agree ___c. Disagree ___d. Strongly disagree ___e. Let's discuss

432. **If my spouse wanted to quit a good-paying job and take a lesser-paying job that he or she enjoyed more, I would not object.**

M: ___a. Strongly agree ___b. Agree ___c. Disagree ___d. Strongly disagree ___e. Let's discuss
F: ___a. Strongly agree ___b. Agree ___c. Disagree ___d. Strongly disagree ___e. Let's discuss

433. **The best way to raise a family is for the wife to stay home full time to take care of the children and have the husband financially support the family.**

M: ___a. Strongly agree ___b. Agree ___c. Disagree ___d. Strongly disagree ___e. Let's discuss
F: ___a. Strongly agree ___b. Agree ___c. Disagree ___d. Strongly disagree ___e. Let's discuss

434. **I expect my spouse to work full time, whether or not we had children.**

M: ___a. Strongly agree ___b. Agree ___c. Disagree ___d. Strongly disagree ___e. Let's discuss
F: ___a. Strongly agree ___b. Agree ___c. Disagree ___d. Strongly disagree ___e. Let's discuss

435. **A woman, regardless of marital status, should spend her money on whatever she wants.**

M: ___a. Strongly agree ___b. Agree ___c. Disagree ___d. Strongly disagree ___e. Let's discuss
F: ___a. Strongly agree ___b. Agree ___c. Disagree ___d. Strongly disagree ___e. Let's discuss

436. A man, regardless of marital status, should spend his money on whatever he wants.

M: ___a. Strongly agree ___ b. Agree ___c. Disagree ___d. Strongly disagree ___e. Let's discuss
F: ___a. Strongly agree ___ b. Agree ___c. Disagree ___d. Strongly disagree ___e. Let's discuss

437. It is important to have a will and to keep it up to date.

M: ___a. Strongly agree ___ b. Agree ___c. Disagree ___d. Strongly disagree ___e. Let's discuss
F: ___a. Strongly agree ___ b. Agree ___c. Disagree ___d. Strongly disagree ___e. Let's discuss

438. It is important for a husband and wife to each have life insurance.

M: ___a. Strongly agree ___ b. Agree ___c. Disagree ___d. Strongly disagree ___e. Let's discuss
F: ___a. Strongly agree ___ b. Agree ___c. Disagree ___d. Strongly disagree ___e. Let's discuss

439. Leaving a $5 tip on a $30 restaurant bill is too high a tip, even if the food and service were excellent.

M: ___a. Strongly agree ___ b. Agree ___c. Disagree ___d. Strongly disagree ___e. Let's discuss
F: ___a. Strongly agree ___ b. Agree ___c. Disagree ___d. Strongly disagree ___e. Let's discuss

NOTE: *Answer the following two questions only if you now have children from a previous marriage.*

440. If I remarried, I would make up a new will leaving everything to my new spouse; I would leave nothing to my children.

M: ___a. Strongly agree ___ b. Agree ___c. Disagree ___d. Strongly disagree ___e. Let's discuss
F: ___a. Strongly agree ___ b. Agree ___c. Disagree ___d. Strongly disagree ___e. Let's discuss

441. If I remarried, I would make up a new will in which I would split my estate between my new spouse and my children.

M: ___a. Strongly agree ___ b. Agree ___c. Disagree ___d. Strongly disagree ___e. Let's discuss
F: ___a. Strongly agree ___ b. Agree ___c. Disagree ___d. Strongly disagree ___e. Let's discuss

Household Duties

Do you enjoy having a clean home? Do you take pride in working hard to make your home pleasant and attractive? Do you believe in hiring other people (house cleaners, gardeners) to keep your house in tiptop shape? Or would you rather spend your time and money on other, less-mundane, endeavors?

DIRECTIONS: **IF you are a male,** place your check mark next to the response that most closely matches how much you agree or disagree with each statement. Select "Let's discuss" *only* if you believe the other answers are not appropriate. Place your checkmark in the row opposite the "M," which stands for "male." **IF you are a female,** follow the same directions, except place your checkmark on the row marked "F" for "female."

442. I would expect my partner to take care of the *inside* of the house (cleaning, decorating), and I would take care of the *outside* of the house (such as painting, raking leaves, emptying garbage).

M: ___a. Strongly agree ___ b. Agree ___ c. Disagree ___ d. Strongly disagree ___ e. Let's discuss
F: ___a. Strongly agree ___ b. Agree ___ c. Disagree ___ d. Strongly disagree ___ e. Let's discuss

443. I enjoy cleaning my home.

M: ___a. Strongly agree ___ b. Agree ___ c. Disagree ___ d. Strongly disagree ___ e. Let's discuss
F: ___a. Strongly agree ___ b. Agree ___ c. Disagree ___ d. Strongly disagree ___ e. Let's discuss

444. I enjoy repairing things around the house.

M: ___a. Strongly agree ___ b. Agree ___ c. Disagree ___ d. Strongly disagree ___ e. Let's discuss
F: ___a. Strongly agree ___ b. Agree ___ c. Disagree ___ d. Strongly disagree ___ e. Let's discuss

445. I am not good at making household repairs, but I'd rather *try* to fix things myself than have to pay someone to fix them.

M: ___a. Strongly agree ___ b. Agree ___c. Disagree ___d. Strongly disagree ___e. Let's discuss
F: ___a. Strongly agree ___ b. Agree ___c. Disagree ___d. Strongly disagree ___e. Let's discuss

446. I once deliberately smashed something I was trying to repair because the repair was just not going right.

M: ___a. Strongly agree ___ b. Agree ___c. Disagree ___d. Strongly disagree ___e. Let's discuss
F: ___a. Strongly agree ___ b. Agree ___c. Disagree ___d. Strongly disagree ___e. Let's discuss

447. It drives me crazy to see someone throw clothes on the floor.

M: ___a. Strongly agree ___ b. Agree ___c. Disagree ___d. Strongly disagree ___e. Let's discuss
F: ___a. Strongly agree ___ b. Agree ___c. Disagree ___d. Strongly disagree ___e. Let's discuss

448. It is important to clean one's home every day.

M: ___a. Strongly agree ___ b. Agree ___c. Disagree ___d. Strongly disagree ___e. Let's discuss
F: ___a. Strongly agree ___ b. Agree ___c. Disagree ___d. Strongly disagree ___e. Let's discuss

449. Couples are so busy these days that the only sensible approach to cleaning the house is to hire someone else to do it.

M: ___a. Strongly agree ___ b. Agree ___c. Disagree ___d. Strongly disagree ___e. Let's discuss
F: ___a. Strongly agree ___ b. Agree ___c. Disagree ___d. Strongly disagree ___e. Let's discuss

450. I like having a clean home.

M: ___a. Strongly agree ___ b. Agree ___c. Disagree ___d. Strongly disagree ___e. Let's discuss
F: ___a. Strongly agree ___ b. Agree ___c. Disagree ___d. Strongly disagree ___e. Let's discuss

451. Messy homes make me uncomfortable.

M: ___a. Strongly agree ___ b. Agree ___c. Disagree ___d. Strongly disagree ___e. Let's discuss
F: ___a. Strongly agree ___ b. Agree ___c. Disagree ___d. Strongly disagree ___e. Let's discuss

452. Doing the laundry is the woman's responsibility.

M: ___a. Strongly agree ___ b. Agree ___ c. Disagree ___d. Strongly disagree ___e. Let's discuss
F: ___a. Strongly agree ___ b. Agree ___ c. Disagree ___d. Strongly disagree ___e. Let's discuss

453. Extremely clean homes make me uncomfortable.

M: ___a. Strongly agree ___ b. Agree ___ c. Disagree ___d. Strongly disagree ___e. Let's discuss
F: ___a. Strongly agree ___ b. Agree ___ c. Disagree ___d. Strongly disagree ___e. Let's discuss

Relatives

Are you close to your relatives? Or have they forgotten your name? (Perhaps it's because you moved and left no forwarding address?)

Some of your relatives may be like the rarest of gemstones (they add value and richness to your life) while others may be like pieces of road tar on the bottom your shoe (you can't shake them off at your doorstep).

When you involve your partner in your life, your relatives (legally or socially) become your partner's relatives; this may be cause for celebration...or a reason to leave town!

DIRECTIONS: **IF you are a male,** place your check mark next to the response that most closely matches how much you agree or disagree with each statement. Select "Let's discuss" *only* if you believe the other answers are not appropriate. Place your checkmark in the row opposite the "M," which stands for "male." **IF you are a female,** follow the same directions, except place your checkmark on the row marked "F" for "female."

454. I like my relatives (most of them).

M: ___a. Strongly agree ___ b. Agree ___ c. Disagree ___d. Strongly disagree ___e. Let's discuss
F: ___a. Strongly agree ___ b. Agree ___ c. Disagree ___d. Strongly disagree ___e. Let's discuss

Relatives

455. I *don't* like my relatives (most of them).

M: ___a. Strongly agree ___ b. Agree ___c. Disagree ___d. Strongly disagree ___e. Let's discuss
F: ___a. Strongly agree ___ b. Agree ___c. Disagree ___d. Strongly disagree ___e. Let's discuss

456. Just because someone is related to you doesn't mean you have to associate with them.

M: ___a. Strongly agree ___ b. Agree ___c. Disagree ___d. Strongly disagree ___e. Let's discuss
F: ___a. Strongly agree ___ b. Agree ___c. Disagree ___d. Strongly disagree ___e. Let's discuss

457. If a parent causes an adult child too much pain, the adult child may have to "divorce" the parent. ("Divorce" in this case means to permanently end the parent/child relationship.)

M: ___a. Strongly agree ___ b. Agree ___c. Disagree ___d. Strongly disagree ___e. Let's discuss
F: ___a. Strongly agree ___ b. Agree ___c. Disagree ___d. Strongly disagree ___e. Let's discuss

458. It doesn't matter what a relative does to you, you should still respect all your relatives.

M: ___a. Strongly agree ___ b. Agree ___c. Disagree ___d. Strongly disagree ___e. Let's discuss
F: ___a. Strongly agree ___ b. Agree ___c. Disagree ___d. Strongly disagree ___e. Let's discuss

459. If my parent or an in-law became too involved in my personal affairs, I would cut that person out of my life.

M: ___a. Strongly agree ___ b. Agree ___c. Disagree ___d. Strongly disagree ___e. Let's discuss
F: ___a. Strongly agree ___ b. Agree ___c. Disagree ___d. Strongly disagree ___e. Let's discuss

460. It's important that the roles of in-laws be identified and agreed upon in the early stages of a marriage.

M: ___a. Strongly agree ___ b. Agree ___c. Disagree ___d. Strongly disagree ___e. Let's discuss
F: ___a. Strongly agree ___ b. Agree ___c. Disagree ___d. Strongly disagree ___e. Let's discuss

461. If my parents became too involved in my relationship or my life, I would tell them to leave me alone.

M: ___a. Strongly agree ___ b. Agree ___c. Disagree ___d. Strongly disagree ___e. Let's discuss
F: ___a. Strongly agree ___ b. Agree ___c. Disagree ___d. Strongly disagree ___e. Let's discuss

462. I think it is important for adult children to be emotionally and financially independent of their parents.

M: ___a. Strongly agree ___ b. Agree ___c. Disagree ___d. Strongly disagree ___e. Let's discuss
F: ___a. Strongly agree ___ b. Agree ___c. Disagree ___d. Strongly disagree ___e. Let's discuss

463. If my in-laws became too involved in my relationship or my life, I would tell them to leave me alone.

M: ___a. Strongly agree ___ b. Agree ___c. Disagree ___d. Strongly disagree ___e. Let's discuss
F: ___a. Strongly agree ___ b. Agree ___c. Disagree ___d. Strongly disagree ___e. Let's discuss

464. I believe parents and parents-in-law should never give advice unless their children ask for it.

M: ___a. Strongly agree ___ b. Agree ___c. Disagree ___d. Strongly disagree ___e. Let's discuss
F: ___a. Strongly agree ___ b. Agree ___c. Disagree ___d. Strongly disagree ___e. Let's discuss

465. I would appreciate the advice of my parents or parents-in-law.

M: ___a. Strongly agree ___ b. Agree ___c. Disagree ___d. Strongly disagree ___e. Let's discuss
F: ___a. Strongly agree ___ b. Agree ___c. Disagree ___d. Strongly disagree ___e. Let's discuss

466. I would not mind having any one (or both) of my parents living with my partner and me if they needed to do so.

M: ___a. Strongly agree ___ b. Agree ___c. Disagree ___d. Strongly disagree ___e. Let's discuss
F: ___a. Strongly agree ___ b. Agree ___c. Disagree ___d. Strongly disagree ___e. Let's discuss

467. I would not mind having any one (or both) of my *in-laws* living with my partner and me if they needed to do so.

M: ___a. Strongly agree ___ b. Agree ___c. Disagree ___d. Strongly disagree ___e. Let's discuss
F: ___a. Strongly agree ___ b. Agree ___c. Disagree ___d. Strongly disagree ___e. Let's discuss

468. I would not mind living with my parents or parents-in-law if we (as a couple) were having money problems.

M: ___a. Strongly agree ___ b. Agree ___c. Disagree ___d. Strongly disagree ___e. Let's discuss
F: ___a. Strongly agree ___ b. Agree ___c. Disagree ___d. Strongly disagree ___e. Let's discuss

469. I enjoy helping out my relatives.

M: ___a. Strongly agree ___ b. Agree ___c. Disagree ___d. Strongly disagree ___e. Let's discuss
F: ___a. Strongly agree ___ b. Agree ___c. Disagree ___d. Strongly disagree ___e. Let's discuss

470. I would resent having to help my relatives.

M: ___a. Strongly agree ___ b. Agree ___c. Disagree ___d. Strongly disagree ___e. Let's discuss
F: ___a. Strongly agree ___ b. Agree ___c. Disagree ___d. Strongly disagree ___e. Let's discuss

471. I would resent having to help out my spouse's relatives.

M: ___a. Strongly agree ___ b. Agree ___c. Disagree ___d. Strongly disagree ___e. Let's discuss
F: ___a. Strongly agree ___ b. Agree ___c. Disagree ___d. Strongly disagree ___e. Let's discuss

472. I would help anyone if they truly needed it.

M: ___a. Strongly agree ___ b. Agree ___c. Disagree ___d. Strongly disagree ___e. Let's discuss
F: ___a. Strongly agree ___ b. Agree ___c. Disagree ___d. Strongly disagree ___e. Let's discuss

473. If my parents did not approve of my partner, I would end my relationship with that partner.

M: ___a. Strongly agree ___ b. Agree ___c. Disagree ___d. Strongly disagree ___e. Let's discuss
F: ___a. Strongly agree ___ b. Agree ___c. Disagree ___d. Strongly disagree ___e. Let's discuss

474. If my parents did not approve of my partner, I would politely listen to their concerns and then continue seeing my partner.

M: ___a. Strongly agree ___ b. Agree ___c. Disagree ___d. Strongly disagree ___e. Let's discuss
F: ___a. Strongly agree ___ b. Agree ___c. Disagree ___d. Strongly disagree ___e. Let's discuss

475. If my parents did not approve of my partner, I would consider their concerns and evaluate my relationship with my partner. I would then make my own decision as to whether or not to continue my relationship with my partner.

M: ___a. Strongly agree ___ b. Agree ___c. Disagree ___d. Strongly disagree ___e. Let's discuss
F: ___a. Strongly agree ___ b. Agree ___c. Disagree ___d. Strongly disagree ___e. Let's discuss

476. If my parents did not approve of my partner, I would tell them to mind their own business.

M: ___a. Strongly agree ___ b. Agree ___c. Disagree ___d. Strongly disagree ___e. Let's discuss
F: ___a. Strongly agree ___ b. Agree ___c. Disagree ___d. Strongly disagree ___e. Let's discuss

477. It may not be a good idea to discuss my marital problems with my parents because they may hold a grudge against my partner once the problems are resolved.

M: ___a. Strongly agree ___ b. Agree ___c. Disagree ___d. Strongly disagree ___e. Let's discuss
F: ___a. Strongly agree ___ b. Agree ___c. Disagree ___d. Strongly disagree ___e. Let's discuss

478. I enjoy attending social gatherings of relatives.

M: ___a. Strongly agree ___ b. Agree ___c. Disagree ___d. Strongly disagree ___e. Let's discuss
F: ___a. Strongly agree ___ b. Agree ___c. Disagree ___d. Strongly disagree ___e. Let's discuss

479. During a social gathering of relatives, I try to find a quiet corner to wait until it's time to go home.

M: ___a. Strongly agree ___ b. Agree ___c. Disagree ___d. Strongly disagree ___e. Let's discuss
F: ___a. Strongly agree ___ b. Agree ___c. Disagree ___d. Strongly disagree ___e. Let's discuss

Children

Kids. Ya gotta love 'em, right? You're not normal if you don't want children, right? *WRONG!* People should more carefully weigh the decision of having or not having children and not bend to the pressure of parents, friends, and relatives to procreate. Being a parent is one of the toughest jobs around. It's not for everyone.

Children

DIRECTIONS: **IF you are a male,** place your check mark next to the response that most closely matches how much you agree or disagree with each statement. Select "Let's discuss" *only* if you believe the other answers are not appropriate. Place your checkmark in the row opposite the "M," which stands for "male." **IF you are a female,** follow the same directions, except place your checkmark on the row marked "F" for "female."

480. I have children.

M: ___ a. Yes ____ b. No c. ____ Let's discuss
F: ___ a. Yes ____ b. No c. ____ Let's discuss

481. Kids are nice to have around.

M: ___a. Strongly agree ___ b. Agree ___c. Disagree ___d. Strongly disagree ___e. Let's discuss
F: ___a. Strongly agree ___ b. Agree ___c. Disagree ___d. Strongly disagree ___e. Let's discuss

482. I had a happy childhood.

M: ___a. Strongly agree ___ b. Agree ___c. Disagree ___d. Strongly disagree ___e. Let's discuss
F: ___a. Strongly agree ___ b. Agree ___c. Disagree ___d. Strongly disagree ___e. Let's discuss

483. I want to have children in the future.

M: ___a. Strongly agree ___ b. Agree ___c. Disagree ___d. Strongly disagree ___e. Let's discuss
F: ___a. Strongly agree ___ b. Agree ___c. Disagree ___d. Strongly disagree ___e. Let's discuss

484. I do not want to have any children (or any more children).

M: ___a. Strongly agree ___ b. Agree ___c. Disagree ___d. Strongly disagree ___e. Let's discuss
F: ___a. Strongly agree ___ b. Agree ___c. Disagree ___d. Strongly disagree ___e. Let's discuss

485. I would consider adopting children.

M: ___a. Strongly agree ___ b. Agree ___c. Disagree ___d. Strongly disagree ___e. Let's discuss
F: ___a. Strongly agree ___ b. Agree ___c. Disagree ___d. Strongly disagree ___e. Let's discuss

486. If my partner and I had trouble conceiving a child, I would not hesitate to try every procedure available, no matter how involved or expensive, to help us have a baby.

M: ___a. Strongly agree ___ b. Agree ___c. Disagree ___d. Strongly disagree ___e. Let's discuss
F: ___a. Strongly agree ___ b. Agree ___c. Disagree ___d. Strongly disagree ___e. Let's discuss

487. There is nothing wrong with spanking children.

M: ___a. Strongly agree ___ b. Agree ___c. Disagree ___d. Strongly disagree ___e. Let's discuss
F: ___a. Strongly agree ___ b. Agree ___c. Disagree ___d. Strongly disagree ___e. Let's discuss

488. The father should be the one to discipline the children.

M: ___a. Strongly agree ___ b. Agree ___c. Disagree ___d. Strongly disagree ___e. Let's discuss
F: ___a. Strongly agree ___ b. Agree ___c. Disagree ___d. Strongly disagree ___e. Let's discuss

489. Teenagers need to be firmly disciplined at all times.

M: ___a. Strongly agree ___ b. Agree ___c. Disagree ___d. Strongly disagree ___e. Let's discuss
F: ___a. Strongly agree ___ b. Agree ___c. Disagree ___d. Strongly disagree ___e. Let's discuss

490. Teenage rebellion is a normal stage of growth.

M: ___a. Strongly agree ___ b. Agree ___c. Disagree ___d. Strongly disagree ___e. Let's discuss
F: ___a. Strongly agree ___ b. Agree ___c. Disagree ___d. Strongly disagree ___e. Let's discuss

491. If my teenage daughter became pregnant, I would kick her out of the house.

M: ___a. Strongly agree ___ b. Agree ___c. Disagree ___d. Strongly disagree ___e. Let's discuss
F: ___a. Strongly agree ___ b. Agree ___c. Disagree ___d. Strongly disagree ___e. Let's discuss

492. I enjoy children, no matter what age they are.

M: ___a. Strongly agree ___ b. Agree ___c. Disagree ___d. Strongly disagree ___e. Let's discuss
F: ___a. Strongly agree ___ b. Agree ___c. Disagree ___d. Strongly disagree ___e. Let's discuss

493. If my teenage son fathered a child, I would kick him out of the house.

M: ___a. Strongly agree ___ b. Agree ___c. Disagree ___d. Strongly disagree ___e. Let's discuss
F: ___a. Strongly agree ___ b. Agree ___c. Disagree ___d. Strongly disagree ___e. Let's discuss

Children

494. If I married a person with children, I wouldn't mind playing the role of parent to those children.

M: ___a. Strongly agree ___b. Agree ___c. Disagree ___d. Strongly disagree ___e. Let's discuss
F: ___a. Strongly agree ___b. Agree ___c. Disagree ___d. Strongly disagree ___e. Let's discuss

495. I understand that children often experience problems in accepting a new step-parent.

M: ___a. Strongly agree ___b. Agree ___c. Disagree ___d. Strongly disagree ___e. Let's discuss
F: ___a. Strongly agree ___b. Agree ___c. Disagree ___d. Strongly disagree ___e. Let's discuss

496. If I were a step-parent, I would expect that I would discipline the children as if they were my own.

M: ___a. Strongly agree ___b. Agree ___c. Disagree ___d. Strongly disagree ___e. Let's discuss
F: ___a. Strongly agree ___b. Agree ___c. Disagree ___d. Strongly disagree ___e. Let's discuss

497. If I married a person with grandchildren, I wouldn't mind playing the role of grandparent to those children.

M: ___a. Strongly agree ___b. Agree ___c. Disagree ___d. Strongly disagree ___e. Let's discuss
F: ___a. Strongly agree ___b. Agree ___c. Disagree ___d. Strongly disagree ___e. Let's discuss

498. In raising me, my parents made some mistakes that I will not repeat in raising my own children.

M: ___a. Strongly agree ___b. Agree ___c. Disagree ___d. Strongly disagree ___e. Let's discuss
F: ___a. Strongly agree ___b. Agree ___c. Disagree ___d. Strongly disagree ___e. Let's discuss

499. If my partner physically or emotionally abused our child, or *any* child, I would end the relationship if my partner did not seek counseling to stop the abusive behavior.

M: ___a. Strongly agree ___b. Agree ___c. Disagree ___d. Strongly disagree ___e. Let's discuss
F: ___a. Strongly agree ___b. Agree ___c. Disagree ___d. Strongly disagree ___e. Let's discuss

500. If my partner sexually abused our child, or *any* child, I would end our relationship.

M: ___a. Strongly agree ___b. Agree ___c. Disagree ___d. Strongly disagree ___e. Let's discuss
F: ___a. Strongly agree ___b. Agree ___c. Disagree ___d. Strongly disagree ___e. Let's discuss

III. THE FUTURE

You may have matched in every area, and *then* you find out that your partner's life goal is to become a host on a home shopping channel, while you dream of going to Russia to help spread capitalism! You never know. You just never know.

DIRECTIONS: **IF you are a male,** place your check mark next to the response that most closely matches how much you agree or disagree with each statement. Select "Let's discuss" *only* if you believe the other answers are not appropriate. Place your checkmark in the row opposite the "M," which stands for "male." **IF you are a female,** follow the same directions, except place your checkmark on the row marked "F" for "female."

501. I would like to travel around our state (or province).

M: ___a. Strongly agree ___b. Agree ___c. Disagree ___d. Strongly disagree ___e. Let's discuss
F: ___a. Strongly agree ___b. Agree ___c. Disagree ___d. Strongly disagree ___e. Let's discuss

502 I would like to travel around the country.

M: ___a. Strongly agree ___b. Agree ___c. Disagree ___d. Strongly disagree ___e. Let's discuss
F: ___a. Strongly agree ___b. Agree ___c. Disagree ___d. Strongly disagree ___e. Let's discuss

503. Someday, I would like to travel to different parts of the world.

M: ___a. Strongly agree ___b. Agree ___c. Disagree ___d. Strongly disagree ___e. Let's discuss
F: ___a. Strongly agree ___b. Agree ___c. Disagree ___d. Strongly disagree ___e. Let's discuss

504. Someday, I would like to move out of the city or town in which I currently live and live elsewhere in the state/province.

M: ___a. Strongly agree ___b. Agree ___c. Disagree ___d. Strongly disagree ___e. Let's discuss
F: ___a. Strongly agree ___b. Agree ___c. Disagree ___d. Strongly disagree ___e. Let's discuss

505. I would like to move to another part of the country someday.

M: ___a. Strongly agree   ___ b. Agree   ___c. Disagree   ___d. Strongly disagree   ___e. Let's discuss
F: ___a. Strongly agree   ___ b. Agree   ___c. Disagree   ___d. Strongly disagree   ___e. Let's discuss

506. I would like to retire soon.

M: ___a. Strongly agree   ___ b. Agree   ___c. Disagree   ___d. Strongly disagree   ___e. Let's discuss
F: ___a. Strongly agree   ___ b. Agree   ___c. Disagree   ___d. Strongly disagree   ___e. Let's discuss

507. I would like to retire at an age younger than 65.

M: ___a. Strongly agree   ___ b. Agree   ___c. Disagree   ___d. Strongly disagree   ___e. Let's discuss
F: ___a. Strongly agree   ___ b. Agree   ___c. Disagree   ___d. Strongly disagree   ___e. Let's discuss

508. I don't think I will ever retire; I enjoy my work too much.

M: ___a. Strongly agree   ___ b. Agree   ___c. Disagree   ___d. Strongly disagree   ___e. Let's discuss
F: ___a. Strongly agree   ___ b. Agree   ___c. Disagree   ___d. Strongly disagree   ___e. Let's discuss

509. I don't think I will ever retire; I don't think I could afford it.

M: ___a. Strongly agree   ___ b. Agree   ___c. Disagree   ___d. Strongly disagree   ___e. Let's discuss
F: ___a. Strongly agree   ___ b. Agree   ___c. Disagree   ___d. Strongly disagree   ___e. Let's discuss

510. If I had someone to support me, I would quit my job and stay home.

M: ___a. Strongly agree   ___ b. Agree   ___c. Disagree   ___d. Strongly disagree   ___e. Let's discuss
F: ___a. Strongly agree   ___ b. Agree   ___c. Disagree   ___d. Strongly disagree   ___e. Let's discuss

511. If I had someone to support me, I would quit my job and take a lower-paying, more personally satisfying job.

M: ___a. Strongly agree   ___ b. Agree   ___c. Disagree   ___d. Strongly disagree   ___e. Let's discuss
F: ___a. Strongly agree   ___ b. Agree   ___c. Disagree   ___d. Strongly disagree   ___e. Let's discuss

512. Someday I would like to marry (or if previously married, married again).

M: ___a. Strongly agree   ___ b. Agree   ___c. Disagree   ___d. Strongly disagree   ___e. Let's discuss
F: ___a. Strongly agree   ___ b. Agree   ___c. Disagree   ___d. Strongly disagree   ___e. Let's discuss

513. I would like to continue my schooling.

M: ___a. Strongly agree ___ b. Agree ___c. Disagree ___d. Strongly disagree ___e. Let's discuss
F: ___a. Strongly agree ___ b. Agree ___c. Disagree ___d. Strongly disagree ___e. Let's discuss

514. I would like to obtain a college degree in a field that is different from my current field.

M: ___a. Strongly agree ___ b. Agree ___c. Disagree ___d. Strongly disagree ___e. Let's discuss
F: ___a. Strongly agree ___ b. Agree ___c. Disagree ___d. Strongly disagree ___e. Let's discuss

515. I would like to quit my current job and obtain another one.

M: ___a. Strongly agree ___ b. Agree ___c. Disagree ___d. Strongly disagree ___e. Let's discuss
F: ___a. Strongly agree ___ b. Agree ___c. Disagree ___d. Strongly disagree ___e. Let's discuss

516. I would like to take some evening courses in subjects that interest me.

M: ___a. Strongly agree ___ b. Agree ___c. Disagree ___d. Strongly disagree ___e. Let's discuss
F: ___a. Strongly agree ___ b. Agree ___c. Disagree ___d. Strongly disagree ___e. Let's discuss

517. It would bother me to be alone as I grow older.

M: ___a. Strongly agree ___ b. Agree ___c. Disagree ___d. Strongly disagree ___e. Let's discuss
F: ___a. Strongly agree ___ b. Agree ___c. Disagree ___d. Strongly disagree ___e. Let's discuss

Congratulations! You've almost completed the questionnaire! Here's the final statement:

518. A relationship is like a living thing; it needs care and attention, or it will wither and die. Nothing is easier than to take a loved one for granted and to believe that the love will always be there, no matter what. It takes *work* to keep love alive; but the effort is worth it, for there are few joys greater than to be with the one you love.

M: ___a. Strongly agree
F: ___a. Strongly agree

(Author's note: Forgive me; I seemed to have run out of toner in my printer just as I was typing the above answer lines...)

NOW WHAT?

Now, if you and your partner have each completed the questions you agreed to complete, compare your answers.

If you both agreed on a statement, but agreed on it by different degrees (for example, "Agree" versus "*Strongly* agree"), don't worry about it. You at least know how your partner stands on an issue. However, you may wish to discuss those statements in which one partner selected "Agreed" or "Strongly agreed" and the other selected "Disagreed" or "Strongly disagreed."

You should make every effort to discuss those statements that one or both of you marked "Let's discuss." This book opened the door to the discussion, and now it's your turn to follow through.

If you find it difficult to discuss sensitive issues, you might try a tip that has worked for me: Write each other letters. (Really!) You may find it easier to sit down and take the time to express thoughts on paper. There are no verbal interruptions and no instant adjustment of your words in reaction to your partner's behavior. It may also be easier for your partner to take the time to read and digest your words and to write a thought-out response, instead of offering a quick verbal reply.

Another tip: If you are planning a wedding, it may be a good idea to add "See a marital therapist" to your long list of things to do, even if you were previously married. Does this sound crazy to you? Well, think about it — every day, a marital therapist sees people who are in the middle of "marital war zones." Such a therapist may help *you* avoid being a casualty by providing you with valuable insight into your own relationship.

If you are looking for assistance in maintaining your relationship, you will find an abundance of self-help books available at your local library or bookstore. You may also wish to find a counselor or therapist who specializes in your particular concern. It's not always easy to find a therapist with whom you are comfortable, but don't give up. There are plenty of good professional people who want to help you. You may also find support groups helpful. Check your local newspaper for meeting announcements or try the phone book.

Take a look at the "Resources" section of this book for information sources on topics relating to love and relationships.

Be Careful

Don't make the mistake of showing this questionnaire to your partner years from now when it seems as if someone may have been fibbing on a few questions. Dishonesty may not be the case.

Human behavior *cannot* be accurately predicted. You can make assumptions, but you never know what a person will do. The human being is an ever-changing creature. The person you marry today may **not** be the person you are still married to in two or ten or thirty years from now — mentally, physically, or emotionally.

Values often change as a person grows older. The things people value at age 21 usually do not hold the same importance at ages 41 or 61. Your answers to this questionnaire reflect the values you hold *today*.

We all change; sometimes these changes guide us in the same direction — and sometimes we take vastly different paths.

This book serves only as a tool to enlighten you about the person who may become an important part of your life. *Good luck on your road to happiness!*

BONUS QUIZ!   Take the following quiz to test your knowledge about AIDS.*

Directions: On the line below (or on a separate paper), write "T" next to the statements you think are true, and "F" next to the statements you think are false. The answers are on the next page.

___ 1.   (True or False) Most of the people in the world who are infected with HIV are gay males.

___ 2.   (True or False) Most HIV-infected people or people with AIDS in the U.S. are members of racial minority groups.

___ 3.   (True or False) Worldwide, one million children are infected with HIV.

___ 4.   (True or False) In the next six years, worldwide, an estimated 5 to 10 million children under the age of 10 will be orphaned as a result of the AIDS-related deaths of their parents.

___ 5.   (True or False) In the U.S., the leading cause of death for males between the ages of 25 and 44 is prostrate cancer.

___ 6.   (True or False) In the U.S., the fastest-growing rate of cases of AIDS is in the 13- to 24-year-old age group.

___ 7.   (True or False) AIDS ranks eighth among the top ten most common fatal diseases in the United States.

___ 8.   (True or False) Worldwide, three percent of all people infected with HIV are female.

___ 9.   (True or False) If you have sex without properly using a condom, you place yourself at risk for AIDS exposure.

*This quiz was developed from data received from the American Foundation for AIDS Research. Statistics are current as of 11/93.

ANSWERS to AIDS Quiz:

1. **FALSE**. Worldwide, 75% of all HIV-infected people were exposed to the virus through unprotected heterosexual sex.
2. **FALSE**. In the U.S., White Americans account for 55% of all adult AIDS cases; African Americans account for 25%; and Latino/Latina Americans, 16%.
3. **TRUE**.
4. **TRUE**.
5. **FALSE**. In the U.S., the leading cause of death for males between the ages of 25 and 44 is AIDS.
6. **TRUE**.
7. **TRUE**.
8. **FALSE**. Worldwide, 40% of all people infected with HIV are female.
9. **TRUE**.

NOTE FROM THE AUTHOR:

Everybody says: "It won't happen to me..."
But it can happen to *anybody*.
Having sex without using a condom is one
way you place yourself at risk.
Please take precautions. Get tested. Use condoms.
Be careful.
Life is precious.

Resources

Books:

Barbach, Lonnie and David L. Geisinger. *Going The Distance.* Doubleday. 1992. ISBN. 0-385-26112-8.

Beattie, Melodie. *Codependent No More - How To Stop Controlling Others and Start Caring for Yourself.* Hazelden/HarperCollins. 1987. ISBN 0-06-255446-8.

DeAngeles, Barbara. *Are You The One For Me?* Island Books, Dell Publishing, 1992. ISBN 0-440-215-15-7.

Forward, Susan and Torres, Joan. *Men Who Hate Women and The Women Who Love Them.* Bantam Books. 1986. ISBN 0-553-26507-5.

Hendrix, Harville. *Getting The Love You Want.* Harper Perennial.1988. ISBN 0-06-097292-0.

Hendrix, Harville. *Keeping the Love You Find.* Pocket Books, Simon & Schuster, Inc. 1992. ISBN 0-671-73419-9.

Sills, Judith. *How To Stop Looking For Someone Perfect and Find Someone To Love.* Ballantine Books. 1984. ISBN 0-345-32597-4.

Resources (continued)

Any book by Dr. Ruth Westheimer, including:

Westheimer, Ruth K. and Louis Lieberman. *Dr. Ruth's Guide to Erotic and Sensuous Pleasures.* Shapolsky Publishers, Inc., New York, 1991. ISBN 1-56171-035-0.

Westheimer, Ruth K. *Dr. Ruth's Guide For Married Lovers.* Warner Books, Inc., 1986. ISBN 0-446-51282-6.

Westheimer, Ruth K. *Dr. Ruth's Guide to Good Sex.* Warner Books, Inc. 1983.

AIDS Information:

For more information about HIV/AIDS, call the National AIDS Hotline Centers for Disease Control at 1-800-342-AIDS
Also: 1-800-344-7432 (Spanish)
      1-800-243-7889 (TDD/Deaf Access)

To receive a packet of AIDS information, write:

> AIDS Packet
> PO Box 6003
> Rockville, MD 20849

Marital And Family Therapy Referral Service:

American Association For Marital And Family Therapy, 1-800-374-2638. Call this number, and you will be sent a list of therapists in your area who are members of the association.

Index

L

lesbian women, tolerance of, 25
lingerie, 60
lovemaking (see also *Sex* and *Romance*)
    frequency, 51-52
    suggestions for improvement, 55

M

marijuana, tolerance for use of, 45
marital therapy, 49
marriage
    history, 19-20
    plans, 94, 106
masturbation, 55-56

O

oral sex, 53-54
orgasm, 55

P

pets, 78-81
pregnancy, 58, 59
parents, role in adult life, 98-99
politics, 14-16

R

race, 23-25
relatives, 16, 74, 97, 101
religion, 9-13, 26
retirement, 106
romance, 65-68

S

self-esteem, 27
sex (see also *Lovemaking* and *Romance*) 51-64
    abuse, 61, 62
    anal, 54
    fantasies, 62
    frequency, 51-52
    gadgets, 61
    games, 61
    masturbation, 55

sex (continued)
    molesters, 62-63
    oral, 53, 54
    orgasm, 53
    suggestions for improveme
    therapy, 55
sexually transmitted diseases, 57-60
shopping, 71
smoking, 41-43
social skills, 73, 101
sports, 91
step-parents, 103, 104
stress, handling of, 49

T

TV viewing, 69
therapy, 49
tolerance, 23-28, 49

V

vacations, 71-72
violence, 47-50, 61-62, 215

Please write to me!

I would love to hear from you. Tell me what you think of this book. Which questions would you like to see deleted? Do you have any questions you'd like to see added in a future edition? Did this book make a difference in your relationship?

My address is:

> Lorilyn Bailey
> c/o LORMAX Communications
> P.O. Box 40304
> Raleigh, NC 27629-0304

Thank you!

♥

📖 Do you know anyone who might benefit from this book? Or would you like to give copies as gifts? If so, use the order form on the next page.

💾 *The Original LOVERS QUESTIONNAIRE Book* is also available in software on 3-1/2" disks for IBM and IBM-compatible computers!

The software will provide you with several options, including comparisons of your responses, a print-out of those areas in which you disagree or need to discuss further, *and* an opportunity for you to write any comments you may have about the statement after you select your response.

This high-quality, well-designed program is only $39.95, plus shipping, handling and applicable sales tax.

♥

(Makes a great shower gift!)

MAIL YOUR ORDER TO:

LORMAX Communications
PO BOX 40304
Raleigh, NC 27629-0304

(PLEASE PRINT.)

Name_____
Street_____Apt_____
City_____
State_____ Zip_____

Please select the items you wish to order:

Qty: Description   Total

__ The Original **Lovers' Questionnaire** Book @$ 9.95 each   _____
__ The Original **Lovers' Questionnaire** Software* @ $39.95 each   _____
   *Windows®

                 For shipping & handling, add $4.75:   _____

                        NC residents add 6%   _____
                              TOTAL: _____

Please make check or money order payable to: LORMAX Communications.

For Charge Orders:

CALL 1-800-828-6772
Visa, MasterCard,
American Express, EuroCard

NOTE: This book is available at group discount rates.
       Please write to the above address for information.

♥

A big hug and kiss to those,
in the past,
who offered me support and encouragement:

Central North Carolina: Stephen Bailey, Kay Gramiak, Ben Gramiak, Pete and Margie Blair, Bob and Shelba Marsh, Jan and Dennis Wallace, Lane Peele, Susan and Larry Gibson, Jim Buck and Debbie Wutz, Jay Cooper, Theresa Bradford; Molly Foxlady; Raleigh Chamber Roundtable group; Raleigh Singles Club; The Raleigh Big Apple/New York Club.
Western New York: Susan Bates, Sandy and Jeff Allaire, Pam and Bob Dolan, Fran and John Lipani, Lois Tipton and Simon Pontin, Ginnie Bacheler, Dr. Fred Ruckdeschel, Dr. Clint Wallington, Dr. and Mrs. Raymond Gramiak; Class of '73 gang: Robin Longo, Michele and Randy Strauchen, Jan Gardner, Roseanne Baconcini, Patty Steele; Marcy and George Waheibi; Mindy and Wayne Shaffer; Candy and Dan Walters, Deborah Onslow, Maria and Ira Stein, Diep Chu, Janet Lomax, Ida Morse, Fran Henry, John Bartholomay, Ross Incardone, Tammy Fedigan, Dr. Louis Buttino, Judith Lemoncelli, Nancy Keucher, Jeff and Kim Halter, Joan and Fred Barthelmann, Christa Roesner, and Helene Snihur. **Central Florida:** Bruce Barnard. **Southern California:** Stanley Ralph Ross. **Northern California:** Randy Stahl. **Southern England:** Maureen Rizzo. **Northern Japan:** Michael and Susan Unher.
...and to the late Beverly Halter and Joanne Barnard who are so often in my thoughts.

Thanks, too, to the good folks at Night Owl Graphics, Wake County Public Libraries, Cloth World, and the Wal-mart Photo guys in Raleigh, NC.

♥

WHAT THE EXPERTS SAY...

"Explore this book *before* you consider marriage."

Steven Gage, M.A.
Marital Therapist

"Provides ample questions on all aspects of interpersonal relations...an invaluable resource."

Rev. John Dromazos

"...helps even established couples learn more about each other."

Dr. Michael Zande
Psychologist